GREAT AGES OF MAN

A History of the World's Cultures

ANCIENT EGYPT

by

LIONEL CASSON

and

The Editors of TIME-LIFE Books

TIME-LIFE BOOKS, NEW YORK

TIME-LIFE BOOKS

FOUNDER: Henry R. Luce 1898-1967

Editor-in-Chief: Hedley Donovan
Chairman of the Board: Andrew Heiskell
President: James R. Shepley
Chairman, Executive Committee: James A. Linen
Editorial Director: Louis Banks
Group Vice President: Rhett Austell

Vice Chairman: Roy E. Larsen

EDITOR: Jerry Korn
Executive Editor: A. B. C. Whipple
Planning Director: Oliver E. Allen
Text Director: Martin Mann
Art Director: Sheldon Cotler
Chief of Research: Beatrice T. Dobie
Director of Photography: Melvin L. Scott
Assistant Text Directors: Ogden Tanner, Diana Hirsh
Assistant Art Director: Arnold C. Holeywell

PUBLISHER: Joan D. Manley
General Manager: John D. McSweeney
Business Manager: John Steven Maxwell
Sales Director: Carl G. Jaeger
Promotion Director: Paul R. Stewart
Public Relations Director: Nicholas Benton

GREAT AGES OF MAN
SERIES EDITOR: Russell Bourne
Editorial Staff for *Ancient Egypt:*
Editor: Harold C. Field
Assistant Editor: Carlotta Kerwin
Text Editors: Anne Horan,
Paul Trachtman, L. Robert Tschirky
Designer: Norman Snyder
Staff Writers: Peter Chaitin, Leon Greene,
Gerald Simons, Edmund White
Picture Research: David Bridge
Text Research: Barbara Ballantine,
Mary W. Constant, Patricia Skinner,
Linda Wolfe, Susan Apple

EDITORIAL PRODUCTION
Production Editor: Douglas B. Graham
Quality Director: Robert L. Young
Assistant: James J. Cox
Copy Staff: Rosalind Stubenberg,
Renni Browne, Florence Keith
Picture Department: Dolores A. Littles,
Patricia Maye
Art Assistants: Anne Landry, Robert Pellegrini,
Leonard Wolfe

THE AUTHOR: Lionel Casson, Professor of Classics at New York University, is an authority on life in ancient civilizations. He is the author of many books, including *The Ancient Mariners: Seafarers and Sea Fighters of the Mediterranean in Ancient Times* and *Masters of Ancient Comedy.* Professor Casson lectured on classical civilization on the *Sunrise Semester* television series, and from 1963 to 1965 was director of the summer session in classics at the American Academy in Rome.

THE CONSULTING EDITOR: Leonard Krieger, formerly Professor of History at Yale, now holds the post of Professor of History at Columbia University. Dr. Krieger is the author of *The German Idea of Freedom* and *The Politics of Discretion,* and co-author of *History,* written in collaboration with John Higham and Felix Gilbert.

THE COVER: King Khafre, builder of the second pyramid at Gizeh, reflects in his proud face the majesty of ancient Egypt. The statue was carved about 2540 B.C.

The following individuals and departments of Time Inc. gave valuable aid in the preparation of this book: Editorial Production, Norman Airey, Nicholas Costino Jr.; Library, Peter Draz; Picture Collection, Doris O'Neil; Photographic Laboratory, George Karas; TIME-LIFE News Service, Murray J. Gart; Correspondents Mohamed Wagdi (Cairo), Ann Natanson (Rome), Katharine Sachs (London), Elisabeth Kraemer (Bonn), Maria Vincenza Aloisi (Paris).

CONTENTS

Note: The artists and present locations of all works of art reproduced in this book are listed on page 187.

INTRODUCTION

For many people ancient Egypt is a baffling phenomenon. Certainly it is impressive, with its mighty monuments, its three thousand years of history, and its reputation for vast learning and skill. On the other hand, a culture of now deserted monuments, of aloof statues, of a flat and static art and of gaping mummies never seems to pulse with good red blood. We feel no kinship to the austere King Khafre in the Cairo Museum or to Queen Hatshepsut masquerading as Osiris in the Metropolitan Museum. The story of ancient Egypt seems more like a fable than like human history.

This is an unfortunate impression created by a people which, in seeking to find eternity, established a static and unchanging form in art and architecture and thereby obscured their little souls. Those little souls were alert, gay, noisy, romantic and artistic. The Egyptians were like their statues, in which the bland stereotype of the eternally youthful and serene noble overlies the individuality of a firm jaw or a hooked nose. One has to excavate the Egyptian from his covering.

We who feel so little spiritual relation to the ancient Egyptian still use his things, as we sit on a four-legged chair at a four-legged table, writing with a pen on a piece of paper. Such legacies from Egypt and Babylonia have survived for five thousand years. In these respects we are closer to the ancients than to our children who use posture chairs, tape recorders and punch cards, and to our grandchildren, who may use a 13-month calendar. The pace of our lifetime is so fast that we are discarding a long heritage without much consideration.

The Hebrews, the Greeks and the Romans were much impressed by ancient Egypt, and some of them paid respectful credit to that culture for learning and skill. If we are closer in understanding to the Hebrews, the Greeks and the Romans, we must remember that the Egyptians established the essentials of their culture two thousand years before these later peoples. A grandfather may seem hopeless when confronting a stalled motorcar or cranky television set; yet he may have been highly skilled in dealing with horses and a cranky hand pump. Certainly the Egyptian culture must have had the stability which comes from successful adaptation to environment; otherwise the same expression could not have survived for three thousand years.

To us it is a paradox that a tomb, solemnly designed for eternal bliss, should be the setting of lively and gay scenes. Should one carry into the presence of the gods a noisy gang of romping children, a mischievous ape, chattering workmen and a woman guest who has overeaten at a banquet? Should hymns to the gods be loaded with atrocious puns? Should a myth represent the supreme deity as sulking in his arbor because another god challenged his wisdom? These apparent frivolities are as much a part of this gifted people as the stunning accomplishment of the Great Pyramid.

It is the great merit of Lionel Casson's treatment that he sees the Egyptians as people who really did live and love and hate and hope and suffer. He presents them honestly as people who possessed no mystic and lost lore, but who achieved great things by honest effort and, in other respects, fell short of greatness—and who are thus understandable to us in our groping days.

JOHN A. WILSON

Professor of Egyptology, University of Chicago

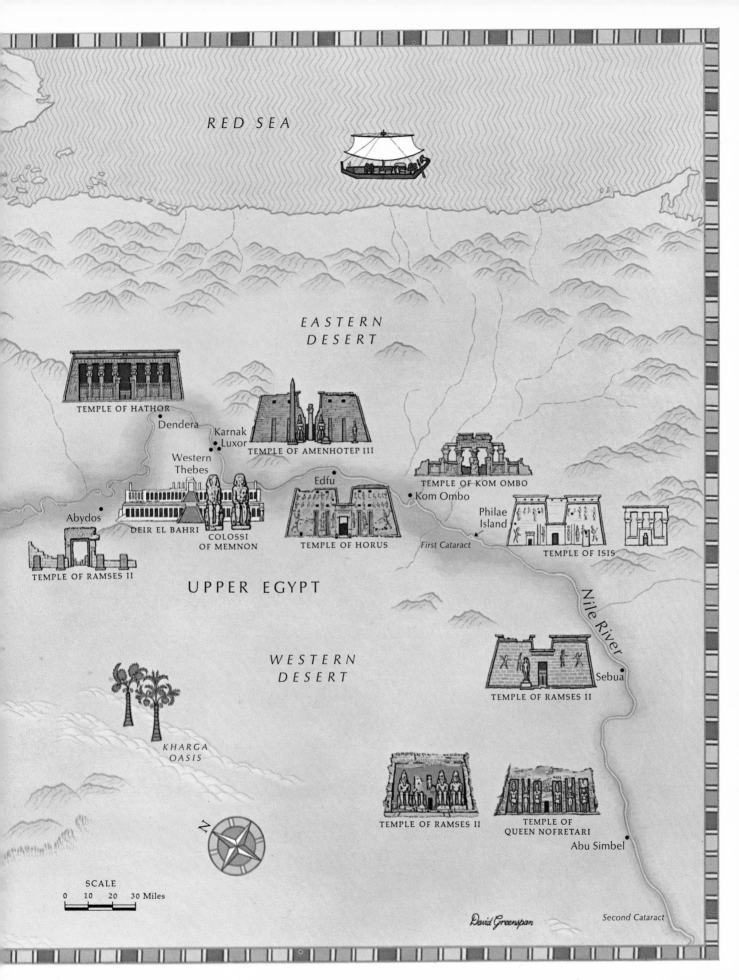

RED SEA

EASTERN
DESERT

TEMPLE OF HATHOR

Dendera

Karnak
Luxor

TEMPLE OF AMENHOTEP III

Western
Thebes

Edfu

TEMPLE OF KOM OMBO

Kom Ombo

Abydos

DEIR EL BAHRI

COLOSSI
OF MEMNON

TEMPLE OF HORUS

Philae
Island

First Cataract

TEMPLE OF ISIS

TEMPLE OF RAMSES II

UPPER EGYPT

Nile River

WESTERN
DESERT

TEMPLE OF RAMSES II

Sebua

KHARGA
OASIS

N

SCALE
0   10   20   30 Miles

TEMPLE OF RAMSES II

TEMPLE OF
QUEEN NOFRETARI

Abu Simbel

David Greenspan

Second Cataract

1

THE ENDURING LAND

Antiquity, vast and richly textured, cloaks the land of Egypt. In the dimness of prehistory, more than 10,000 years ago, man began to settle in the long valley ribboned by the Nile. Sustained by the life-giving river, the land prospered and, in the Fourth Millennium before Christ, burst into splendor under the first of the pharaohs. And in splendor outstanding in the ancient world, it flourished for 27 centuries.

Egypt was ancient even to the ancients. It was a great nation a thousand years before the Minoans of Crete built their palace at Knossos, about 900 years before the Israelites followed Moses out of bondage. It flourished when tribesmen still dwelt in huts above the Tiber. It was viewed by Greeks and Romans of 2,000 years ago in somewhat the same way the ruins of Greece and Rome are viewed by modern man.

The great Greek historian Herodotus made a grand tour of ancient Egypt in the Fifth Century B.C. and wrote of "wonders more in number than those of any other land and works it has to show beyond expression great." Later writers bore him out. Journeying the Nile, they passed the imposing mounds of the pyramids, avenues of sphinxes, slender obelisks. They were dwarfed by towering images in stone and intrigued by enigmatic hieroglyphics covering the walls of temples.

Modern man knows of many ancient and wonderful civilizations, some of them of misty origin and impressive accomplishments. What sets Egypt apart from the others?

For one thing, Egypt was one of the earliest of the ancient lands to weave the threads of civilization into a truly impressive culture. More to the point, it sustained its achievements unabated for more than two and a half millennia—a span of accomplishment with few equals in the saga of humanity.

Nature favored Egypt. The early civilizations of Mesopotamia stood on an open plain, and they spent much of their vitality in defending themselves from one another. Palestine, farther west, was largely unprotected, prey to invaders. In Egypt it was different. Desert barriers girded the Valley of the Nile and discouraged invasion; the people lived in relative security. The scattered tribes that

A SYMBOL OF ROYALTY, *this perfectly preserved amulet was among the treasures found in Pharaoh Tutankhamen's tomb. Tutankhamen was of the 18th Dynasty, one of the 30 dynasties of kings that ruled Egypt for 3,000 years.*

shared the river merged into villages instead of fighting among themselves; the villages learned to cooperate in controlling the river's annual flood so that all might reap abundant harvest.

Cooperation meant organization. And it was the gift for organization, perhaps more than any other single factor, that enabled Egypt to erect a dominant, enduring state.

The first important move in this direction occurred around 3100 B.C. At that time the Egyptian people, hitherto divided into two lands, Upper and Lower Egypt, found themselves under a single monarch—the first of 30 dynasties of pharaohs. They thereby became the world's first united nation and took a decisive step toward establishing a stable civilization. With the first two dynasties, which covered some 400 years, Egypt emerged from prehistoric obscurity into the full light of history. From that point on are numbered its greatest centuries. They are divided into three main eras—the Old Kingdom, the Middle Kingdom and the New Kingdom, separated by two intermediate periods when the country's fortunes were temporarily at low ebb.

Each of the three Kingdoms was characterized by accomplishments of its own. The Old Kingdom, from about 2700 B.C. to 2200 B.C., was the period during which the great pyramids were built. With the Middle Kingdom, about 2000 B.C. to 1800 B.C., Egypt enjoyed an expanding political strength and broader economic horizons. The New Kingdom, beginning about 1600 B.C., saw the nation's zenith as a political power and its acquisition of an empire mostly in Asia. When the New Kingdom came to a close around 1100 B.C., Egypt's days as a great nation were over, although pharaohs, interspersed with foreign conquerors, continued to occupy the throne until the Fourth Century B.C.

The unique quality of Egyptian civilization began to emerge even under the earliest pharaohs.

Political and social structure quickly crystallized into the form it was to maintain, with few interruptions, from then on. All power, in theory and to a great extent in fact, lay in the hands of the ruler. Cast in the double role of king and god, he sat enthroned at the pinnacle of society. Supporting him were the high officers to whom he delegated authority. Below them, the ranks of a vast bureaucracy rested upon the broad shoulders of workers and peasants.

The awakening of Egypt was accompanied by the introduction of writing, all-important prerequisite to successful centralized rule. Records could now be kept, instructions issued, history written down. The creators of poems, stories, essays and narratives could now entrust their works to papyrus rather than memory, and Egypt's literature was born. Methods of calculating kept pace with writing. It became possible to compute taxes with precision, to survey land, measure weights and distances, and reckon time.

Medical science may be said to have begun in Egypt. Though their knowledge was at times tainted with magic, the Egyptian doctors and surgeons of antiquity achieved international renown, and with some cause. Hippocrates of Cos, who fathered modern medicine in the Fifth Century B.C., and the famous Roman anatomist Galen, about 700 years later, both admitted a debt to Egypt.

With all power emanating from a single fountainhead, manpower could be amassed to tame the Nile. Under the first pharaohs, irrigation projects were launched on a grand scale; a spreading network of canals carried water to the fields, and dike systems held the river at bay and reclaimed thousands of arable acres.

As the Nile's green fringe of agriculture grew ever greater, so did the material wealth of its civilization. By 2600 B.C., Egyptian trading vessels bearing cargoes of lentils, textiles, papyrus and other

SOARING TWIN PILLARS *tower over Karnak's ruins. One is decorated with the lotus plant of Upper Egypt (left) and the other with Lower Egypt's papyrus. Together they symbolize the union of the two lands.*

native products were venturing regularly into the Red Sea and the eastern Mediterranean. Overland traders penetrated deep into Nubia's hinterland to the south. Cities flourished beside the Nile, enriched by the treasures of Africa and the ancient East—copper, bronze, gold and silver, ivory and rare woods, lapis lazuli and turquoise, myrrh and spices, exotic animal skins and ostrich plumage.

With spectacular suddenness, an architecture sprang up that was suitable for kings and gods. Within a century after the first pharaoh of the Old Kingdom mounted his throne, Egyptian builders had graduated from sun-baked bricks to highly sophisticated construction in stone, and their artisans were among the earliest to master this difficult technique. The same omnipotent authority that drafted mass labor for irrigation was able to recruit unlimited sinew to quarry and dress enormous blocks, and to transport them to sites beside the Nile. Within a brief span of 200 years or so, Egypt's builders had so mastered the new material that they had finished the pyramids at Gizeh, wonders of the ancient world and the mightiest royal sepulchers of all time. In succeeding centuries, Egyptian architects flanked the river from the Delta, near the Mediterranean, to lower Nubia, about 800 miles south, with stone monuments that rank with the most impressive of any age.

Art kept pace with architecture. From prehistoric days, craftsmen of the Nile had displayed a sense of beauty and symmetry that touched even the most utilitarian objects—flint knives, stone or pottery household vessels, pins and combs of bone or shell. With the advent of the pharaohs, this esthetic quality flowered into a mature art, distinctively Egyptian in concept and character. For the next 3,000 years, Egypt produced a graceful and spirited art (that served, among other things, to inspire the great Greek sculptors and artists who followed them centuries later).

Sculptors carved colossal images of impassive gods or rulers in stone, and also fashioned life-sized portraits in stone, wood and copper. Painters added vivid pigments to the works of the sculptors —and also covered temple walls with stately official and religious scenes, and decorated palaces and tombs with animated frescoes. The important buildings of the ancient Egyptians were brilliant with color.

Travelers from abroad who reached the Valley of the Nile long after its civilization had passed its zenith saw the Egyptians as mysterious, unfathomable. Later ages, drawing conclusions from silent tombs and gigantic monuments, speculated that they must have been a gloomy, oppressed people, preoccupied by thoughts of death and forever hauling huge blocks under the cutting whip of the overseer.

It was, we know now, a totally false picture. Far from being morbid or downtrodden, the Egyptians were sociable and lighthearted, and among the most industrious of ancient peoples. Enamored of life on earth, they envisioned death merely as its happy continuance.

And life, on the whole, was good in Egypt under the pharaohs. On occasion it was upset by war, political unrest or famine, but in normal times its course flowed serenely. The lot of the peasantry, though hard, was not without its compensations. An Egyptian peasant certainly knew more security and had fewer worries than his counterpart in lands periodically laid waste by conquerors. It is true that his day was spent toiling in another man's fields. But the soil he served provided him and his family with sustenance, though it was usually frugal, and the river was liberal with its fish. During the months when the Nile flood made the fields untillable, he might have been drafted for labor in the quarries or on one of the pharaoh's projects. On the other hand, floodtime was festival time,

when all work paused long enough for him to join in celebrating great religious feasts.

From his humble mud-brick home beside the Nile, the peasant might look across the river, busy with its traffic of boats and barges, to where workmen swarmed about some half-completed edifice. Most of the workers—the masons, carpenters and minor artisans—lived as simply and frugally as the peasants did. The sculptors, painters, cabinetmakers and other specialists who would add a temple's finishing touches knew a higher standard of living, in prosperous times at least. Their dwellings, like those of the middle-class government bureaucracy, might rise to two stories and embrace a small garden.

The nobleman who controlled the land that the peasant worked often lived in considerable luxury. If he was a high-ranking official, his town or country house—made of the sun-baked brick the Egyptians used for all domestic architecture, from hovels to palaces—was usually set in a landscaped garden enclosed by a high wall. Its whitewashed elegance and columned veranda were reflected in a large pool stocked with fish and scattered with lotus blossoms. Visitors were greeted in a central reception hall about which were clustered smaller public rooms, guest rooms and the family's private chambers. Comfortable furnishings—couches, tables, chairs, beds, chests and colorful wall hangings —attested to the competence of Egypt's craftsmen.

Those who dwelt within the royal palace itself enjoyed a life of splendor. Through broad courts, frescoed halls and corridors friezed with faïence tiles flowed a constant stream of imperial business. Shaven-headed priests, high dignitaries and army officers came and went on matters of domestic, foreign and religious concern. Subject princes from Syria and Palestine arrived, often accompanied by dazzling retinues. Upon a dais in a lofty, colonnaded audience hall the god-king sat enthroned,

SIZING UP THE SPHINX, *two French scientists measure its great head in this sketch by artist Vivant Denon, who accompanied Napoleon's army. The French, like many earlier conquerors, were awestruck by Egypt's architectural splendors. Recalling the arrival of the French at Luxor in 1799, Denon wrote, "the army, at the sight of its scattered ruins, halted of itself and, by one spontaneous impulse, grounded its arms."*

flanked by a bodyguard and attended by ranks of courtiers. Here he received ambassadors from the courts of Babylonia, Crete, the Hittites and other nations; here he accepted rich tribute brought by newly conquered chieftains in exotic dress.

Set apart from the pageantry of state were the pharaoh's private apartments—his robing chamber, bedroom and bath, and the adjoining quarters of the royal harem. Opening off the apartments was the Balcony of Appearances. From this vantage point, on festive or solemn occasions, the monarch displayed himself to crowds in a court below, and from it he bestowed gifts and decorations upon deserving retainers.

Though extremely remote in time, the civilization of ancient Egypt is in some respects more intimately known today than that of any other nation of antiquity. The Old Testament is rich in references to Egypt. In addition, history and literature written by the Egyptians themselves have endured in the stone of temples, monuments and tombs, and on papyrus scrolls.

The fundamental conservatism of the ancient Egyptians also helped preserve the evidences of their civilization. Although they were subjected to alien rulers in their latter days and assaulted on every hand by foreign influences, they clung tenaciously to the customs and beliefs of their past. Thus many remains of their culture lasted virtually intact almost until modern times, to be observed firsthand and recorded by writers of the rising Western world.

The Egyptians themselves were responsible for the preservation of many artifacts of their civilization because of their distinctive attitude toward death. Since they viewed death as an extension of life, they prepared for it elaborately. Any man who could afford a proper tomb spared neither energy nor expense to furnish it with the many things thought indispensable for living in the hereafter. Geography and climate assisted in the preservation process. Most of the land bordering the Nile is desert, receiving little or no rainfall. The remains of the past, blanketed by dry sand, rested undisturbed through the millennia. Even the most perishable materials—delicate fabrics, articles of fragile wood, papyrus—survived relatively unscathed.

As a result of these two factors—religion and climate—Egypt remained a huge and unique storehouse of antiquity. Its artifacts span all the periods from primitive prehistory to the sophisticated and magnificent age of the pharaohs. Scenes painted on the walls of tombs from dynastic days onward faithfully depict many details of Egyptian life. Their subjects range from the lowly tasks of farmers and servants and the joyous games of children to the pomp and ceremony that attended gods and kings. Small wooden models reproduce dwellings, ships, soldiers in battle gear; butchers, bakers and brewers in their shops. Although the tomb furnishings—

clothing, musical instruments, furniture, cosmetics, tools and weapons—were for the use of the dead, all shed light on the ways of the living.

Nevertheless, in the years that followed the decline of Egypt, it was a long time before anyone saw much by this light. Through the Middle Ages and the Renaissance, the odds and ends of Egyptian antiquities that found their way to Europe were usually regarded merely as puzzling curiosities.

It was not until 1798 when Napoleon launched his conquest of Egypt that the veil began to lift. Accompanying Napoleon's troops was a small array of savants dedicated to a study of the Valley of the Nile. Under their ministrations there began to take shape a picture of a vital people endowed with great skills. The discovery by one of Napoleon's officers of the Rosetta Stone—a fragment of a stele inscribed not only in hieroglyphics but also in an Egyptian script called demotic and in Greek —provided the final key to Egypt's lost history. Its bilingual text made it possible for the philologist Jean François Champollion, who had devoted years to the study of ancient languages, to announce in 1822 that the enigma of the hieroglyphs had been solved: for the first time, the pictographs could be read.

Ancient Egypt had no sooner begun to speak for itself than the unfolding of its tale was abruptly postponed through the action of mindless vandals. A rage for amassing Egyptian antiquities swept Europe. The heritage of the pharaohs was exploited unmercifully; architectural fragments, statues, mummies, papyri and tomb furnishings were carried off wholesale to enrich museums and private collections. In this seller's market, the methods used by relic-hunters were crude, often little better than outright looting. One Italian adventurer-turned-archeologist, for example, bludgeoned his way into tombs with a battering ram and reported that "Every step I took I crushed a mummy in some part or other." What the dry sands had preserved for millennia, human greed and haste were shattering in seconds.

Egyptian authorities at length were persuaded to protect the fast-vanishing legacy of their ancestors. In 1858, at the urging of former consul Ferdinand de Lesseps (the same Frenchman who later cut the canal through Suez), they named an experienced French Egyptologist, Auguste Mariette, first Conservator of Egyptian Monuments. With full control of antiquities in his hands and the backing of the government, Mariette managed to curb the grand-scale plundering of tombs and temples. Through his influence the foundations were laid for the present Cairo Museum, housing treasures of the past.

Yet even Mariette and his French successor Gaston Maspero were by modern standards shockingly careless in excavating important sites. It was not until William Matthew Flinders Petrie, a comparatively unknown and largely self-taught British Egyptologist, arrived in 1880 that digging in Egypt became precise and orderly. To Petrie, archeology was a means not simply of digging for treasure but of re-creating the life of the people, humble as well as great, who had buried their kings amid splendor. Under Petrie, the trowel, camel's-hair brush and record book replaced the battering ram. Howard Carter, an Englishman and former student of Petrie who discovered the tomb of Tutankhamen and its stunning treasure in 1922, learned his lesson from Petrie so well that it took him eight years to record and remove the hundreds of rich furnishings heaped in the tomb's four small chambers.

Since Petrie's day, exacting work by scholars and archeologists of France, Britain, Germany, the United States and other nations has stripped much of the mystery from ancient Egypt. Its peoples and culture now stand revealed in their proper light as one of the great civilizations the world has known.

A MIGHTY BUILDER, *Ramses II is portrayed in huge twin statues at Luxor. Inscribed at right are hieroglyphs of the King's formal names and titles.*

MONUMENTS AND GOD-KINGS

Life everlasting for Egypt's pharaohs was the sustaining principle of Egyptian civilization. In an ancient religious text, a deceased king asks of the creator-god, "O Atum, what is my duration of life?" And the deity replies, "Thou art destined for millions of millions of years, a lifetime of millions."

To supply the necessities for their lifetime of millions, the kings designed tombs and mortuary temples that would last forever. A common designation for tomb, in fact, meant "house of eternity." The people of Egypt willingly labored to build these monuments for their dead rulers, believing that, as gods, the pharaohs had to be properly provided for and propitiated.

Many vast sepulchers and massive shrines survive to this day—some 2,000 years after the culture that created them waned and perished. The tombs have kept alive the names of the ancient kings—fulfilling, in a very real sense, the Egyptian idea that "To speak the name of the dead is to make him live again."

17

A GODLY BEAST
STANDING GUARD

Egyptian civilization was already ancient when the first Greek travelers came to Egypt and discovered, standing at the edge of the desert, the strange limestone beast which they called the Sphinx. This may have been a Greek corruption of the Egyptians' designation of the monument. But nothing like this Sphinx had ever been seen in Greece. The gigantic figure crouching in the sand near the modern village of Gizeh has a lion's body measuring 240 feet long and 66 feet high, and a human face more than 13 feet wide.

Ever since this hybrid creature was given its foreign name, the Great Sphinx at Gizeh has represented to outlanders all that is strange and inscrutable about the civilization of ancient Egypt. Yet, despite the statue's remote origins, a good deal about it has been learned or deduced. Egyptians considered the Sphinx an embodiment of Harmakhis, a manifestation of their sun god. The human features are believed to be a portrait of Khafre, the King of Egypt when the statue was carved.

Nothing about the Great Sphinx is more certain—or harder to comprehend—than its tremendous age. According to an ancient text, a young prince riding in the desert paused to nap in the shade of the Sphinx. As he slept, the Sphinx spoke to him, promising him Egypt's throne if he would remove the sand that had piled up around the statue. The prince, Thutmose IV, did clear the sand and indeed became King of Egypt 34 centuries ago—and at that time the Sphinx was already 1,100 years old.

A HEAD OF DJOSER, *heavily damaged but still revealing, suggests the commanding personality of a great king. In his reign, the size of Egyptian sculpture and architecture dramatically increased.*

DJOSER'S TEMPLE *and step pyramid (background) at Sakkarah, although the first all-stone structures, were nevertheless built along lines used by architects accustomed to working with mud bricks.*

THE LOFTIEST PYRAMIDS, *built at Gizeh for Khufu (right) and Khafre, form a backdrop for a caravan. Camels came into general use in Egypt at least 20 centuries after these tombs were built.*

A GOLDEN AGE MEMORIALIZED IN STONE

Some 4,700 years ago, Egypt entered a period of great technological progress. Until about 2700 B.C., the basic building material had been sun-dried brick. Yet, less than 200 years later, the pyramids at Gizeh had been built of stone blocks which weighed up to 15 tons, and which fitted together with the precision of a necklace clasp *(pages 129-139)*.

The techniques that produced Egypt's monumen-
tal civilization were pioneered by Imhotep, who was Vizier to the powerful King Djoser. At Sakkarah, using small stone blocks instead of traditional mud bricks, Imhotep constructed for Djoser a step-sided pyramid and a rectangular funerary temple. Nothing like these buildings had ever been seen before. Though these structures were soon dwarfed by others, they made a legend of Imhotep's skill.

MASSIVE REMINDERS OF A VIRILE KING

Ramses II, called "the Great," earned that accolade by doing things on a grand scale and with enormous gusto. In an opulent 67-year reign he waged an extravagant war against a coalition of Asian states led by the Hittites, sired more than 100 children, and erected Egypt's biggest and showiest buildings.

Among his monuments were two huge temples cut into the cliffs at Abu Simbel. Recently these structures were involved in a project vast enough to delight the King himself: to save them from sinking beneath the lake created by Aswan High Dam, both were cut apart and re-assembled on higher ground.

GUARDIAN STATUES, *four depicting Ramses II and two of his wife Nofretari, stand in niches flanking the entrance to the Queen's temple, located a few hundred feet north of the King's shrine.*

A GIGANTIC EFFIGY, *one of four 67-foot-high statues of Ramses II, looks out over the Nile River at Abu Simbel. The figures at bottom represent a few members of the immediate royal family.*

23

ROYAL WIVES AND A WILLFUL QUEEN

Egypt's throne was traditionally occupied only by men. Many queens, including the lovely Nefertiti, won great renown as wives to kings, but only a few queens ever ruled in their own right.

The most famous of the women who did reign, Queen Hatshepsut, at first served as regent to her stepson Thutmose III. Even before the prince reached maturity, she completely usurped the reins of government. Flaunting all the trappings of kingship, even male dress and ceremonial false beard, this remarkable woman built a lavish temple (*above*) to keep her name alive. When she fell, after 20 years in power, Thutmose claimed his throne and vengefully destroyed much of her great memorial.

HATSHEPSUT'S TEMPLE, *a complex of col-*
onnaded shrines, rises in terraces to the
cliffs at Deir el Bahri. The chief ex-
ploits of the Queen's reign were de-
picted in carvings along the porticoes.

NEFERTITI'S PORTRAIT, *carved in the*
realistic style used during the reign of
her husband Akhenaton, reveals the
loveliness implied by her name: Nefer-
titi means "the Beautiful One is come."

A FALLEN GRANDEUR

One of the most somber relics of ancient Egypt is an immense unfinished statue of Osiris, Lord of Eternity, which lies today, as it has for over 2,000 years, in a red-granite quarry near the town of Aswan. The exact purpose for which it was carved

and the reason it was never completed are irretrievably lost in the remote past. An abandoned stone god, the statue seems to symbolize the fall of Egypt's great and long-lived civilization. It was just such a statue, one of Ramses II, that inspired the Romantic poet Percy Bysshe Shelley to write his famous lines: "On the sand, / Half sunk, a shattered visage lies . . . / And on the pedestal these words appear: / 'My name is Ozymandias, king of kings: / Look on my works, ye Mighty, and despair!'"

2

THE GIFT
OF THE RIVER

SKILLED MARINERS, *two Egyptian oarsmen maneuver their boat as a crew-man stands between them. Some Egyptian boats were over 200 feet long, and it took expert pilots to cope with the Nile's ever-shifting sandbars.*

The Nile was to ancient Egypt what the sea is to Britain and the Alps are to Switzerland. It fashioned the nation's economy, determined its political structure and created the values it chose to live by.

The river flows more than 4,000 miles in all. Two great streams converge to form it: the Blue Nile, which rises in Ethiopia, and the White Nile, which rises in Uganda. They join at Khartoum to become the Nile proper, and from there the united stream runs 1,900 miles north to the Mediterranean. From Khartoum much of its course is through a valley gashed in desert. It creates in the midst of a sterile land an elongated oasis that for thousands of years has nurtured civilization. The river gave those who lived along it prosperity; the desert that lies beside it gave them security. These two geographical features determined the facts of physical existence for the ancient Egyptian and molded his mental attitudes.

On its course north from Khartoum, the river is interrupted at six points by rapids—the famous Nile Cataracts. The sixth is just downstream from Khartoum itself. The first is at Aswan, and marks the Nile's entry into Egypt proper. From here there is no further interruption until it reaches the Mediterranean. For the last hundred miles or so the river fans out in tributaries over the marshy flats of a delta, so named by the Greeks for its triangular shape, which resembled their letter "delta."

It was in the 750-mile stretch between the First Cataract and the sea that the civilization we know as Egyptian rose and flourished. It is an area divided by geography into two distinctly different regions. The part near the Delta is known as Lower Egypt; the part to the south of it, where the land is more arid and the river is bordered on both sides by frowning cliffs, is known as Upper Egypt.

Each year the main stream of the Nile, swollen with the torrential rains that fall in Ethiopia, rushes north and spreads its waters over Egypt. "When the Nile inundates the land," the Greek Herodotus wrote in the Fifth Century B.C., "all of Egypt becomes a sea, and only the towns remain above water, looking rather like the islands of the Aegean. At such times shipping no longer follows the stream, but goes straight across the country. Anyone, for example, traveling from Naucratis to Mem-

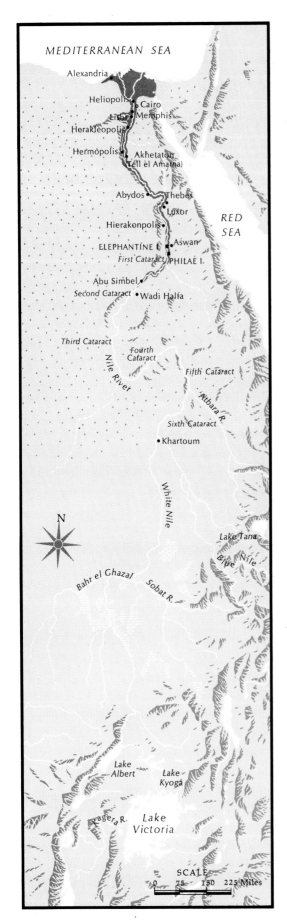

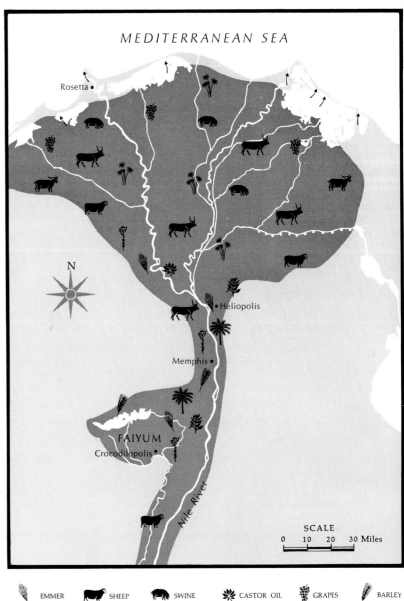

| | EMMER | | SHEEP | | SWINE | | CASTOR OIL | | GRAPES | | BARLEY |
| | CATTLE | | PAPYRUS | | DATE PALM | | FLAX | | SESAME | | GOATS |

EGYPT'S LONG, VERDANT LIFELINE

THE REALM OF THE NILE *(left) extends more than 4,000 miles from its sources deep in Africa to its mouth in the Mediterranean. The earliest Egyptians knew little about the upper reaches of their river, and believed it gushed up from an underground sea at the island of Elephantine near the First Cataract. Actually, three main streams combine to form the great river. The White Nile starts in Lake Victoria, meets the Blue Nile at Khartoum and is joined by the Atbara River another 200 miles downstream. Once in Egypt, the Nile glides past Thebes, a New Kingdom capital, and the rich plain of Faiyum. The Delta, above, was Egypt's rich agricultural center, fanning out beyond the Old Kingdom capital of Memphis. Here a wide variety of crops and livestock thrived in ancient times. The map shows the Delta as it now appears; only vague information is available on its ancient configuration. The sites of the seven mouths of the old river are shown by arrows*

phis sails right alongside the pyramids." When the waters recede, they leave behind a layer of fertile silt—"black land," the Egyptians called it, to distinguish it from the sterile "red land" of the desert.

Egypt is "the gift of the river," Herodotus noted. Without the Nile, the country would have been barren; with it, the pharaohs ruled one of the most richly endowed lands of the age. The Egyptians never had to scan the skies anxiously in search of rain; every summer the Nile provided irrigation. They never had to fear exhausting the soil; every summer the Nile refreshed it.

Like so many of nature's phenomena, the Nile could be a trial as well as a blessing. If the annual flood was too high, the spreading stream wrought havoc; if it was too low, the life-giving waters missed marginal areas, there was less land to sow and food ceased to be plentiful. If a low flood was repeated for several consecutive years, there was famine. Joseph's prediction in the Old Testament of seven fat years and seven lean years reflects what could happen along the Nile. The margin between relief and worry was meager. A few feet higher than usual might mean drowned villages; a few lower might mean short rations.

During remote prehistoric times, the scattered tribes living by the river were probably content to flee when the Nile rose and return to plant haphazardly in the mud. But to feed a sizable and cohesive population, planning was needed. When the Egyptians discovered how to harness the annual flood, they were on the route to becoming a nation. More than 5,000 years ago, before the founding of the First Dynasty, the Egyptians had learned to determine the seasons of the year by the behavior of the river. The seasons were three: "Inundation," the time of flood, approximately from June through September; "Emergence of the fields from the water," which began in October and left the soil moist from then until about February; and "Drought,"

the time that lasted until June, when the cycle was repeated. Out of this observation came the first practicable calendar, and the one from which the modern Western calendar is derived.

From these seasonal divisions also came social organization, for the river and its behavior determined labor assignments. During the Emergence men caught and hoarded the fast-receding waters and planted in the mud. During the Drought they harvested and threshed. During the Inundation, when the fields were flooded, they hauled stones for the pharaoh's building projects.

They built dikes to keep the river from inundating villages; for the purposes of irrigation they laid out big catch basins to trap the water as the flood receded; they dug canals leading from these so that the water could be released to spill over the fields; and they sank wells. They devised nilometers—gauges to measure the rise of the river—and placed one near what is now Cairo and another just below the First Cataract. As they extended the boundary of Egypt, they set up other nilometers farther south—the pharaoh wanted the earliest possible portent of what the national fate would be for the year.

The great river was almost wholly responsible for Egypt's economy. It fed the people and, except for the gold mined in the eastern desert and Nubia, it furnished most of the wealth. It made Egypt from the outset an agricultural nation. It determined all real estate values, for the land was divided into that which always received the benefits of flooding, that which sometimes did and that which never did, and taxes were assessed accordingly. The river determined many of the cases that came into court, for there were incessant wrangles over rights to the use of water. It determined even the accounts men gave of their lives in the hereafter. When an Egyptian faced the tribunal of the afterworld, of equal importance to his avowal that he had not killed or robbed was his declaration that he had not "held up the water in its season" or "built a dam against running water."

The economy the Nile created was such that Herodotus and the authors of the Bible wrote in wonder of the fleshpots of Egypt. Grain was the chief product, and the Nile gave so bountiful a yield that when the country was well administered Egypt was always in a position to export it.

There was another commodity that the river furnished Egypt—one, moreover, that needed but a fraction of the time and toil it took to produce grain. Along the banks of the Nile, and especially in the swamps of the Delta, there grew in profusion the tall reed called papyrus, the bulrushes with which Moses' mother made the boxlike float for her baby. The Egyptians early taught themselves to fashion an excellent type of paper from the stalk of this reed. It was the most convenient writing material available to the ancient world. The Egyptians exported sheets made from papyrus and maintained a lucrative monopoly on the commodity until about the 12th Century A.D., when rag and wood-pulp paper began to displace it.

Papyrus served not only the economy of Egypt, but the culture of the ancient world as well. Because it was lightweight and could be rolled up, it was infinitely more easily handled than the baked-clay tablets of Mesopotamia and helped to spread the knowledge of writing to the rest of the world. By the beginning of the Christian era, from Syria to Spain scribes wrote their letters, bookkeepers their accounts, clerks their records on papyri made in Egypt.

But this did not exhaust the usefulness of the papyrus plant. The fibers, when twisted, made excellent cordage, and a good many of the vessels that sailed the ancient Mediterranean were rigged with ropes of Egyptian papyrus. Along the Nile, all small boats and many fair-sized ones were made from bundles of bound papyrus reeds. In addition, papyrus served to make baskets, boxes, mats, sandals, sieves and stools. The lowly plant, to be had for the mere cutting, was second only to grain among the Nile's gifts.

For certain commodities that their land lacked, the Egyptians had satisfactory or even superior substitutes. The valley was not a particularly good place for timber, but it provided mud that could be dried in the sun, and from this the Egyptians fashioned all their dwellings, from huts to palaces. The valley did not particularly favor the olive, which in most Mediterranean countries was the principal source of oil, but there was abundant castor oil, flaxseed oil and sesame oil to use instead. Oil was an absolute essential for the ancients, serving all the purposes that butter, soap and electricity serve for the modern world. Ancient peoples cooked in it, cleansed themselves with it and burned it in their lamps.

In the Delta, where the flat expanse lent itself to ranching, the landowners grew sleek cattle. Pigs, which need a moist soil, were raised there, and goats were to be found all over, in Upper as well as Lower Egypt. The marshes of the Delta, lined with thickets of papyrus, were havens for all sorts of water birds; and the Egyptians, gliding in reed punts, went fowling with throwing sticks or set traps for geese, ducks and cranes to bring home for fattening in pens.

An economy must have distribution as well as production—the good things for eating and selling that Egypt produced had to be delivered to consumer and customer. Here again the Nile performed nobly. It was a perfect artery of communication. In many ancient countries distribution of products was slow and expensive, because it had to be done overland, on beasts of burden; in Egypt, thanks to the river, it was cheap and quick. The Nile traveled the length of the country and at the Delta—the only

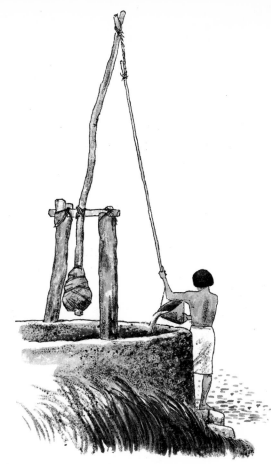

RAISING WATER *from the Nile to fill a walled irrigation ditch, an Egyptian peasant employs a mechanical device called a "shā-dūf." It consists of a long pole balanced on a crossbeam—a rope* *and bucket at one end, a heavy counterweight at the other. By pulling the rope he lowers the bucket into the Nile. Then the counterweight raises the bucket and water is poured into the ditch.*

place where the country was wide—its seven arms provided a web of waterways. Better yet, all the necessary power for locomotion was furnished by the river and the weather. The prevailing wind accommodatingly blows from the north, opposite to the flow of the river; thus a boatman could drift leisurely downriver (or have the crew run out the oars if he was in a hurry) and then raise sail and let the wind waft him back.

As a result of all this, the Nile drew men to its waters at a very early date, thereby making the Egyptians key contributors to the history of water transport. The earliest record of a sail is a picture on an Egyptian pot of about 3200 B.C. Nile boatmen pioneered in the development of river craft. They had reed rafts for nosing through canals and mighty 200-foot barges for hauling obelisks; tiny punts for the everyday task of ferrying and lordly yachts for the grandees; and hulking freighters to carry grain up and down the length of the river.

Pilots, sailors and ferrymen were as important on ancient Egypt's Nile as on Mark Twain's Mississippi. Cross-river traffic was heavy and canals were ubiquitous, so the ferrymen's services were constantly in demand. Ferrymen appear in inscriptions on the pharaohs' tombs. They supplied transport for the royal dead across the waters of the afterworld. Apparently they caused as much trouble in the next life as in this, napping when they were needed, having to be thumped awake, complaining of boat leaks and refusing to go to work.

Politically, the Nile brought Egypt to early unification under a central government. Before the founding of the First Dynasty the groundwork had been laid for corralling and directing of vast manpower; by the time of the First Dynasty, a coordinated effort directed at controlling the waters extended the length of the river. The building and maintaining of dikes, catch basins and canals went on unceasingly, year in and year out, demanding a

THE PATTERN OF THE NILE, *a regular cycle of ebb and flow that remained unchanged for thousands of years, is illustrated on this graph which shows the river flooding to a height of 27 feet at Wadi Halfa in the year 1931-1932, a short time before modern irrigation projects tamed the flow.*

labor force of such size that the only way to enroll it was by conscription—the same system, incidentally, that built the pyramids and the pharaohs' other great monuments. The whole country was involved with the work, for it was of crucial importance. For a stable existence, central authority was of the essence—an authority that could maintain a total effort all along the river, that could store the bounty of a fat year to offset the shortage of a lean year, that could call up and organize and direct the armies of workers required.

Having brought about the need for centralization, the Nile at the same time abetted it by enabling the pharaoh to communicate directly and swiftly with any spot the length of his domain. From his capital, first at Memphis and then later at Thebes, dispatch boats sped upstream and downstream, keeping him in constant touch.

Beyond the river lay two other formations of nature that contributed to Egypt's national fortune and the character of the people: the sea and the desert. Egyptian traders traveled to Punt (probably the coastal area of what is now Somalia), Syria and Lebanon by way of the Red Sea and the Mediterranean, exporting papyrus and linen, importing timber, copper, incense and perfume. The desert slopes were barren of vegetation, but they were rich in excellent hard stone for sculpture, in semiprecious stones such as agate, jasper and amethyst for jewelry, and in gold.

The desert also served Egypt as a deterrent to invasion. The Egyptians could and did go out across it to trade, but others found it difficult to come in. The wasteland to the west is spotted with oases that made caravan traffic possible, but by no means did they form an invasion route. The eastern desert separates the Nile in the north from Palestine and in the south from the Red Sea. The strip along the Red Sea, which is stiffened by a chain of sunbaked, waterless mountains, formed an almost impassable barrier.

To the north Egypt was protected by the Mediterranean Sea, which, like the desert, served for trade but was easily defensible. To the south of Egypt, in Nubia—more or less the northern Sudan of today—the Nile was less bountiful, and the area rarely supported a nation that could threaten the pharaohs. The Nile might have served as a path for invasion were it not for the Cataracts. The pharaohs extended their occupation of Nubia by simply pushing the border from one Cataract to the next and establishing forts along the way.

Nestled within the embrace of such formidable frontiers, Egypt came to nationhood comfortably secure and aloof. Remote from neighbors, the Egyptian dismissed foreigners as having nothing to offer save certain essentials that the valley of the Nile did not provide, such as timber and copper. Sure of his livelihood, he developed an outlook that was cheerful and optimistic.

The upper classes of Egypt led a luxurious life. The ruins of Tell el Amarna, which was founded as a new capital in the 14th Century B.C., reveal the grace and comfort for which the city was built. It spread over a crescent-shaped plain about eight miles long and three miles wide, and was laced with broad boulevards. The palace and the villas of the wealthy stood in the central quarter, which was designed with the demands of the climate well in mind. There were ample gardens, lofty reception rooms decorated with gay murals, balconies oriented toward the evening breeze, and outside sleeping porches, bedrooms, bathrooms with lavatories and basins fed by running water. Even the houses of the most humble had sanitary facilities.

The walls of many tombs depict the life the ancient Egyptians hoped to lead in the hereafter, and it was an extension of the life they led on earth. The wealthy are shown boating on the Nile, fowling in the marshes, picnicking with their families, sipping wine in their cool gardens, lolling in the shade as their field hands gather in a fat harvest. For most hardy ancient peoples the spare diet was the ideal; ancient Egypt, like Dickens' England, went in for the groaning board. On festive occasions meat, fowl, fruit and cakes, washed down with plenty of beer or wine, made up the menu. The guests were scented with perfume and decked with flowers. Flowers abounded, and garlands adorned the festivals. Servants of both sexes, the girls wearing little more than necklace and girdle, waited on the guests; musicians, dancers and singers entertained them.

Egyptian artists added bits of written dialogue to their pictures, much like the balloons in modern comic strips. In one banquet scene a woman tells the servant pouring wine: "Give me eighteen measures! Look—I love it madly!" A servant replies, "Don't worry; I'm not going to leave [the wine jar]." A guest nearby cries: "When is the cup coming around to me?" Another, also waiting her turn, urges all present: "Drink! Bottoms up!" Eat, drink and be merry—and there was no worry about dying because, in the Egyptians' confident conception of destiny, death meant simply a continuation of life's good things. A copy of a minstrel's song inscribed in a tomb of the Third Millennium B.C. says: "The span of earthly things is as a dream; but a fair welcome is given him who has reached the West." (The afterworld was conceived of by Egyptians as being located in the west.)

A considerably later text inscribed on a wooden coffin describes the creator-god as having said: "I made the great inundation that the poor man might have rights therein like the great man." Ancient Egypt by no means had an affluent society; the poor lived in the humblest of homes and they worked all their lives. But so long as the central authority was strong and efficient, few went hungry, and throngs of the humble were regaled at public expense during the holidays, some of which lasted for weeks.

And to judge by the tomb paintings, the gaiety and zest for life were by no means limited to the rich. The artists make abundantly clear the good cheer, the lightheartedness, the fun that was to be found in humble lives. Children romp at boisterous play while the grownups work; two girls have a hair-pulling fight while their companions busily harvest the grain; a field hand sings and beats time while a flutist pipes for a line of reapers; a lone donkey holds up the transport of grain by planting his feet and refusing to budge; comic consternation reigns at a carpentry shop when the foreman drops in unexpectedly. The dialogue is full of raillery, in colloquial Egyptian that is easily translated into modern repartee. "Get a move on!" says one of a gang toting bags of grain. "Hurry up, old man, don't talk so much!" says a porter as he hands over a load of flax to a worker. "The water is rising —it is nearly up to the sheaves." A drover in charge of oxen treading grain coaxes his animals along: "Tread it for your own good—go on, tread for your own good. Your masters get the grain and you can eat the straw. Keep at it!" Stevedores handling cargo boom out, "Watch your step!" at bystanders blocking their way.

Life was cheerful and certain for all, and for the wealthy it was elegant. The Egyptians, pragmatic and easygoing by nature, accepted the bounty of the land unquestioningly. There is no Egyptian contribution to match Hebrew ethics, Greek philosophy or Roman law. For the upper classes the objectives of life were to cut a figure in society, to rise at court, to achieve success (measured in herds of cattle or acres of land), and to be buried in an impressive tomb, appropriately decorated.

The values by which the Egyptians lived can be seen in a piece of literature entitled *The Instruction of the Vizier Ptahhotep*, which was written during the Old Kingdom and studied by hundreds of generations of schoolboys. It purports to be the advice of an aging vizier, the ranking member of the pharaoh's court, to his son. It is full of common sense and observations on the ways of the world. "If thou art one of those sitting at the table of one greater than thyself, take what he may give, when it is set before thy nose. Thou shouldst gaze at what is before thee. Do not pierce him with many stares, [for such] an aggression against him is an abomination. . . . Let thy face be cast down until he addresses thee, and thou shouldst speak [only] when he addresses thee. Laugh after he laughs, and it will be very pleasing to his heart, and what thou mayest do will be pleasing to the heart."

The Old Kingdom would collapse, the Middle Kingdom would grope in the direction of social justice, and the New Kingdom would experience foreign influence and foreign involvement. But the Nile flowed along steadily and surely, its annual life-refreshing flood never failing to arrive when the heat of summer drew near, irrigating the land of the pharaohs, making Egypt one of the most prosperous nations of the ancient world and nourishing a civilization that endured through three millennia of history.

The Egyptians' reverence for the river is evident in the "Hymn to the Nile," which was probably written sometime between the Middle and New Kingdoms for an inundation festival held at Thebes. The following is an excerpt, freely translated.

Hail to thee, O Nile, that issues from the earth and comes to keep Egypt alive! . . . He that makes to drink the desert and the place distant from water. . . .

He who makes barley and brings emmer into being, that he may make the temples festive. If he is sluggish, then nostrils are stopped up, and everybody is poor. If there be thus a cutting down in the food-offerings of the gods, then a million men perish among mortals, covetousness is practiced. . . .

But generations of thy children jubilate for thee, and men give thee greeting as a king, stable of laws, coming forth at his season and filling Upper and Lower Egypt. Whenever water is drunk, every eye is in him, who gives an excess of his good. . . .

If thou art too heavy to rise, the people are few, and one begs for the water of the year. Then the rich man looks like him who is worried, and every man is seen to be carrying his weapons. . . .

When the Nile floods, offering is made to thee, oxen are sacrificed to thee, great oblations are made to thee, birds are fattened for thee, lions are hunted for thee in the desert, fire is provided for thee. And offering is made to every other god, as is done for the Nile, with prime incense, oxen, cattle, birds and flame. . . .

So it is "Verdant art thou!" So it is "Verdant art thou!" So it is "O Nile, verdant art thou, who makest man and cattle to live!"

CROSSING A NILE CANAL *at dusk, a procession of cattle, camels and herders reflects the partnership of man and beast essential to Egyptian life.*

LIFE ON THE NILE

For 5,000 years, the Nile has been the river of life for Egypt and its people. Sustaining existence and supporting a civilization in the desert, it has also rigorously shaped the life of the peasants who have cultivated its shoreland. From the time of the pharaohs, the rhythm of the Nile has effectively divided the people's work year. Through the centuries, men have anxiously watched the annual flooding to learn whether the waters would rise enough to insure irrigation during the growing season. The flood, one ancient writer said, was a time when "the land is in jubilation, then every belly is in joy." The peasant's life has hardly changed at all, although modern dams, regulating the river's flow, have ended the uncertainty about water supply. Ancient ways have persisted. Tools virtually identical with those pictured in ancient tombs still are used. A look at Egypt today faithfully evokes the remote past, and brings to life the round of activities of those who worshipped pharaohs as gods and hailed the Nile as "creator of all good."

THE FERTILE MARGIN

Ancient Egypt, an arid waste of desert extending over thousands of square miles, left man almost nowhere to live but along a thin green strip of land watered by the Nile. As the river flowed from south to north, from the steep cliffs near Aswan to the Delta beyond Cairo, the verdant strip on each

bank varied greatly. In some places it spread over no more than a mile; in other places it covered about 13 miles. In the Delta, a triangular network of river branches, fertile fields, vineyards and orchards extended some 150 miles in width—but even this was a mere strand set against the vast desert be-yond. To the peasants in the fields, the forbidding, inhospita-ble expanse of sand and rock that reached up to the very edge of their villages was a fearful place, lonesome and threatening. The desert was considered the home of the dead, a place for burial. Only in the Nile could they sense the continuity of life.

INGENIOUS AGRICULTURAL TECHNIQUES

Four thousand years ago, one parsimonious Egyptian landowner commanded his son to "Make the most of all my land; strive to the uttermost; dig the ground with your nose in the work." To make the most of the land, Egyptian farmers and field hands had to labor unceasingly. Often it took ingenuity as well as brawn to survive. Farmers used simple tools, but put them to many uses. One large-headed, short-handled implement served to dig and shore up irrigation ditches after the harvest—and then did duty as a hoe during the next planting. Reaping was done by hand with a sickle; the same implement also cut clover for cattle and rushes for making mats. Everyone had to pitch in. Women, though busy with their domestic chores, doubled as field hands. At the harvest everyone poured out into the fields to gather the crop and to celebrate the fact that famine had once more been staved off.

PLOWING THE TOPSOIL *lately deposited by the Nile's flood, a farmer readies the land for planting. Ancient plows barely scratched the surface, for deep plowing would dry the soil.*

WINNOWING WHEAT, *a farmer pitches heavy grain and light chaff up to be separated by the wind. The wooden pitchfork of today is virtually the same as ancient Egyptians used.*

41

SWIFT SAILS AND FORBIDDEN FISH

For pharaohs and peasants alike, the Nile was the main thoroughfare for travel. Because Egypt sprang up along the shores of the Nile, all its cities and towns were easily accessible by boat. Skilled boatwrights developed craft ideally suited to the river. Rigged with broad sails, they could take advantage of the lightest breeze. The boats needed only the simplest harbors; lacking a deep keel, they were easily beached on the sandy riverbank. Curiously, in this river country, eating fish was officially proscribed. Certain fish were the sacred animals of local districts. Those who ate fish were regarded as unclean; the hieroglyph for "abomination" was a fish. To hungry peasants, however, the proscription meant little. They fished often, and a good catch was considered a welcome gift of the river.

LATEEN SAILS BILLOWING, *a small fleet of feluccas heads upstream under the prevailing wind from the north. These swift, light, shallow-draft boats were used both as ferries and as freighters.*

FLINGING WIDE NETS, *two fishermen wade out after a school of fish in the Nile. Ancient nets, made of knotted linen cord with lead weights attached, were closed by pulling a braided drawstring.*

THE HARSH LIFE OF THE VILLAGER

MUD-BRICK HOUSES, *the peasants' thick-walled dwellings were crowded close together. The high slit windows gave inhabitants some privacy.*

The Egyptian village, lying between fertile fields of the riverside and a rust-red expanse of desert, was a crowded, busy center of people eking out a simple existence. For men and women alike, daily rounds of toil lasted from dawn to sunset, with a respite at midday when the sun was too hot to bear. Most men worked in the fields. In times of flood, however, they were drafted for such public works as raising dikes or constructing pyramids.

One writer gave a dour view of peasant life: "Mice abound in the field, locusts descend and animals eat the crop . . . What remains . . . is taken by thieves. The hire of oxen is wasted because the animals have died . . . Then the scribe arrives at the riverbank . . . to register the tax on the harvest."

BAREFOOT WOMEN *carry clay water-jugs to the edge of the Nile. Women who did not live near the Nile got household water from irrigation ditches.*

BAKING BREAD, a woman takes flat loaves from a home oven. Bread was the staple of the peasant's diet; Egyptians had 15 different words for it.

AN IRRIGATION DITCH *brings water to the arid land. New Kingdom Egyptians used a "shā-dūf" (a long beam with a leather bucket at one end and a counterbalance at the other) to raise water from low ditches to higher ones.*

BLINDFOLDED CATTLE *treading in a circle are yoked to the forked wooden centerpost of a primitive water-raising device. The rotating centerpost powered a set of waterwheels that brought water from one ditch to another.*

HARNESSING THE YEARLY FLOOD

In Egypt, a land virtually without rain, irrigation alone made it possible for crops to grow and men to live. One of the earliest official positions in Lower Egypt was that of "canal digger," and one measure of a pharaoh's administration was how much land his engineers could open up to the floodwaters of the Nile. To spread the supply of water, Egyptians caught the flood in immense basins dug out of the earth, and devised primitive but ingenious water-raising mechanisms to get it to where it was needed.

THE MEASURED LAND

A panorama of applied geometry, this Egyptian field is a patchwork of small squares crisscrossed with irrigation canals and ditches. To sustain agriculture in an arid land, the people had to become engineers and learn how to construct

complex irrigation works. To cope with the confusion caused by the annual flood of the Nile, Egyptians worked out the rudiments of geometry. "Rope-stretchers," or surveyors, applied the methods of geometry to redraw property lines ob-

scured during the flood. Thus the needs of agriculture led the ancient Egyptians to become more than good farmers: mastering both the desert and the river, they not only achieved new skills but expanded their intellectual horizons in the process.

3
PATHWAY TO POWER

The age of the pharaohs has no written narrative such as Thucydides supplies for Greek history, Livy for Roman and the Books of Kings for the Hebrews. But it does have information in the tomb inscriptions, paintings on the temple walls, and poetry, prose and state records on preserved papyri. There is also the account of Herodotus, who saw the Egyptian civilization before it had fallen under foreign domination. From all this the general story of what happened under the pharaohs can be pieced together with reasonable accuracy.

It is a story of a strong central government headed by a king who was a god; of a people who sought eternity by envisioning afterlife as a continuation of life on earth, and by devoting much of this life to preparing for the next; of imposing architecture and painting; of a social organization that could conscript all labor and skills for the service of the state.

Some seven or eight thousand years before the birth of Christ, civilization was emerging in scattered areas of the Near East. Man the hunter had become man the settler. He had ceased to depend on the luck of the chase for his food and now fed himself by herding flocks and raising crops instead.

Then suddenly, within a few centuries between 3200 and 3000 B.C., the scattered tribes that lived along the Nile were united under one head, ruled by a formal government. The man who was tribal leader of Upper Egypt (tradition calls him Menes, perhaps another name for a King—Narmer)founded the first of Egypt's 30 dynasties, extended his control northward and united the country.

Menes founded the city of Memphis, 20 miles south of the apex of the Delta, near where the regions of Lower and Upper Egypt meet, and established it as his capital. The city was destined to become the greatest in the land. Menes and his immediate successors—some 18 kings of two successive dynasties that spanned about 400 years—ruled from here, built tombs for their afterlife and knit together the two disparate parts of the kingdom, Lower and Upper Egypt.

With the rise of the Third Dynasty, about 2700 B.C., the era known as the Old Kingdom emerged. During the 500 years that followed, Egypt was peaceful and prosperous, with a pride that bordered

AN ENEMY'S LIKENESS on a temple of Ramses III recalls Egypt's victory over the invading Sea Peoples. To save Egypt from foreign domination, Ramses waged three wars on separate frontiers within six years—and won them all.

on cockiness and with a feeling of complete security. The god-king was supreme. All other Egyptians were his servants—the nobles who staffed his administration as well as the masses who built the canals and dikes that enabled his land to bear crops. The nobility devoted its brains and the peasantry its brawn to raising a mighty, eternal home for the god-king. This was the age that produced the pyramids, the world's first great structures in stone.

The first of the monumental tombs was the Step Pyramid at Sakkarah, which is the necropolis of Memphis; it was built for Djoser, the first Pharaoh of the Third Dynasty. In a burst of active building that followed, the trio of pyramid tombs at Gizeh were reared for the Kings of the Fourth Dynasty: Khufu, Khafre and Menkaure—or Cheops, Chephren and Mycerinus, as they are known in the writings of Herodotus. These are the most famous four out of about 80 pyramids that remain of the many Egypt built during its long history.

With the advent of the Fifth Dynasty came the scent of trouble. First, there were signs of a religious problem: previous to the Fifth Dynasty, the king had been god, a full equal to the other gods; now he was still a god, but the carnate son of the sun god, Re. As Re—and the priests that served him—rose in importance, the power of the god-king diminished. There were signs of economic problems: Egypt had paid no small price to build the pyramids, and now they were costly to maintain. There were signs of political difficulties: the pharaoh's officials, the nobles who served as district governors, became important figures in their own right and a threat to his omnipotence.

This combination of strains grew during the Sixth Dynasty and reached a climax under Pepi II, the last great Pharaoh of the Old Kingdom, who ruled for more than 90 years. When he finally died, centralized rule died with him, and peace and prosperity gave way to disorder and hardship. The or-

SMITING A FOE, *King Narmer, wearing a tall white miter crown as sovereign of the Upper Kingdom, battles to unite Upper and Lower Egypt under his rule. This First Dynasty commemorative palette is one of Egypt's oldest surviving historical records.*

ganization necessary for keeping the Nile harnessed broke down; crops suffered and shortages of food, even occasional famine, plagued Upper Egypt. Asiatic nomads seeped into the Delta and caused continual unrest. The district governors, who had grown in strength during Pepi's long reign, now carved out petty principalities for themselves and quarreled with one another. The Old Kingdom disintegrated, and Egypt entered upon the First Intermediate Period, an unstable feudal age that was to last two centuries.

At Memphis the families of two ephemeral dynasties pretended to rule the land, but beyond their own locality they were scarcely recognized. Two other families arose at Herakleopolis, about 55 miles south of Memphis, and ruled as the Ninth and Tenth Dynasties. All four dynasties were short-lived and each suffered a rapid succession of kings. Finally a fifth family arose at Thebes, a provincial town in a valley far upriver. This

PARADING IN TRIUMPH, *Narmer (at top) wears the captured crown of Lower Egypt on the palette's reverse side. Below him slaves leash two panthers and a bull wrecks an enemy fort. The panthers' necks form a depression in which cosmetics could be ground.*

family vied with and overcame the Herakleopolitans, established themselves as the 11th Dynasty, and extended their sway north. The nation now entered on the era of the Middle Kingdom. In about the year 2000 B.C., with the coming of still another Theban family, who founded the 12th Dynasty, Egypt was once again united.

The kings of the 12th Dynasty maintained an interest in Thebes, but they established their capital at Lisht, about 20 miles south of Memphis. They reorganized the domestic affairs of the country. They curbed the power of the provincial grandees by installing alongside the latter their own dependable Thebans as governors and advisers. Inasmuch as many of the grandees had been entrenched for about 150 years, it was no easy job to supplant their power; it took five kings another 150 years to accomplish it. The 12th Dynasty kings continued the work on canals and dikes and catch basins that were so essential to Egypt's agricul-

tural health. They elevated to national prominence a hitherto obscure deity, Amon, who was to become a mighty force in history; over a millennium and a half later Alexander the Great would invoke his aid in ruling Egypt. They sent a military force into Nubia and pushed Egypt's frontier about 200 miles south, beyond the Second Cataract. The Old Kingdom had taken gold only from the eastern desert; from now on Egypt was to draw a great supply from the Nubian mines. In the north, an expedition made its way deep into Palestine, and Egyptian influence became strong in Palestine and lower Syria. A brisk trade was carried on with these regions by land and by sea, and trade relations extended even as far away as Crete.

The able rulers of the 12th Dynasty restored Egypt to greatness and gave the country much to be proud of: a military reputation, territory to exploit, a wide-ranging foreign trade. These were the paths nearly all future pharaohs were to follow.

But Egypt underwent another setback before reaching the next peak. During the rule of the 13th Dynasty, in the 18th Century B.C., the country entered the Second Intermediate Period, during which there was a long series of ineffectual rulers who provided no central authority. The country seems to have separated at the seam between its two natural geographical parts, Upper and Lower Egypt. The two halves engaged in civil war from time to time, and each half was internally beset by squabbling. At Thebes a regime maintained itself for about two centuries, holding a short strip of territory about 125 miles long between Thebes and the First Cataract. In the south Nubia broke away and in the north a rival to the Theban rule arose, a dynasty founded by foreigners. These were the Hyksos. Egypt, the nation that for so long had had nothing but scorn for neighbors, now endured the humiliation of foreign rule.

Hyksos, which was long translated "shepherd

kings," is today rendered "foreign chieftains." They were Asiatics, probably mostly Semites from Palestine, who filtered in across the desert, settled near the eastern border of Egypt and extended their control over much of the Delta. They could not have had much difficulty overcoming whatever opposition Egypt may have put up, for the Egyptians were not advanced in the arts of war. They fought almost nude; they lugged heavy, unwieldy man-sized shields; and their basic weapons were small axes and feeble bows. The Hyksos, as time went on, introduced new weapons from Asia: body armor, scimitars, effective daggers, powerful bows made of wood and horn, and, most important, horse-drawn chariots. When after about 100 years the Egyptians finally expelled the invaders, they did so by learning to use the foreigners' weapons.

In spite of all their advantages in combat, the Hyksos did not succeed in taking over the whole of the country. Their grip seems to have extended no farther than a point about midway between Memphis and Thebes. Beyond that they were never able to dislodge the Theban regime. This proved their undoing. About the middle of the 16th Century B.C. a vigorous and determined family founded the 18th Dynasty. They built up a powerful army, stormed the mighty fortress the Hyksos had erected in their capital in the eastern Delta, and drove the alien rulers out of the country.

Egypt was once again united. The 18th Dynasty was the first of the New Kingdom. It was destined to make Egypt great in a new way: the pharaohs were from now on to devote their time and effort to foreign conquest and to extend their realm in the south beyond the Fourth Cataract of the Nile and in the northeast to the Euphrates River.

The 18th Dynasty, like the 11th, arose at Thebes, and Thebes is where its story is to be read—in the vast temples the pharaohs erected to the god Amon; in the rock-cut chambers of the Valley of the Kings,

where they laid themselves to rest with splendor; in the cliffs around the valley, which are fairly honeycombed with the tombs of the nobles who served in their administrations. On the walls of temples and tombs, pharaohs and nobles proudly inscribed their accomplishments. These inscriptions are the chief sources for the history of Egypt, and they provide a picture that is reasonably clear.

The first of the great Pharaohs of the New Kingdom was Ahmose I, who expelled the Hyksos and restored to Egypt the boundaries it had held in the Old Kingdom. Amenhotep I, his son, extended the boundary farther south, and he started the country on an era of prosperity that would last for 150 years. Thutmose I, the third Pharaoh of the dynasty, pushed the frontiers farther still, south beyond the Fourth Cataract and northeast to Palestine and Syria.

After the reign of Thutmose I, Egypt's military expansion was suspended for two decades by Thutmose's remarkable daughter, Hatshepsut. She was married to Thutmose II, her half-brother (such marriages among royalty were not unusual; they ensured the legitimacy of the line). When he died after a short rule, she took over the reins of government as regent during the minority of Thutmose III, a child her husband had fathered by a subordinate wife in the harem. Nominally the boy was Pharaoh, and Hatshepsut at first ruled in his name. But she soon abandoned the pretense and established herself as Pharaoh.

Pharaonic Egypt produced a series of exceptional women, of whom Hatshepsut was the most outstanding. Many a pharaoh's queen had had a place in the sun alongside her husband, and two had briefly governed, but Hatshepsut was the first to assume the godship with the kingship and to wear the Double Crown, indicating sovereignty over the two lands of Upper and Lower Egypt. Statues show her in the masculine attire of the kingship;

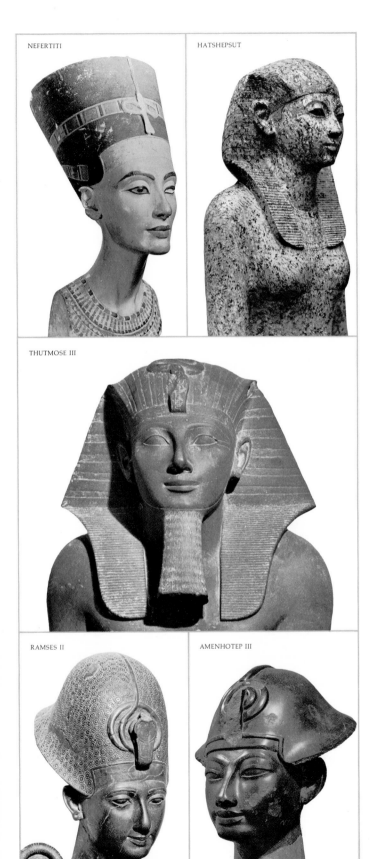

NEFERTITI

HATSHEPSUT

THUTMOSE III

RAMSES II

AMENHOTEP III

PHARAOHS AND QUEENS *of the New Kingdom were often depicted by contemporary artists in busts and statues of basalt, limestone and granite. Five are shown here, in royal headdresses and helmets.*

in some representations she even wears the traditional false beard of the pharaoh. This Pharaoh of the gentle sex forsook battle and returned Egypt to peaceful pursuits: to erecting great monuments and to keeping open the trade routes abroad. The latter had been closed during the Hyksos rule.

Hatshepsut could not have done all she did alone. She obviously had the help of powerful supporters. One in particular was a certain Senmut, who held, according to some accounts, more than 80 different official titles and who must have been her most trusted assistant. As Minister of Public Works, Senmut was in charge of building his mistress' mortuary temple—which was, like all other royal monuments, constructed during her lifetime and under her direction. To get himself a share in her eternal blessedness, Senmut ingeniously sneaked carvings of his own image onto some carefully selected, though unobtrusive, walls. Pharaohs had been known to commemorate their court favorites on the walls of their monuments, but for an official to arrogate a part of a royal temple unto himself was unprecedented. Senmut naturally got his comeuppance; when Hatshepsut discovered his impudence she sent wreckers to mutilate his tomb and smash his sarcophagus. They even managed to ferret out and efface most of the images he had surreptitiously put in his mistress' temple.

One of the surest proofs of Hatshepsut's greatness was her ability to keep a man of Thutmose III's dimensions under her thumb for so long. Thutmose had brains, vision and drive; he was to become the Alexander the Great of Egypt, the creator of Egypt's empire. Yet for 20 years he lived in the shadow of the strong-minded woman who was both his stepmother and his aunt. Finally he gathered the backing he needed to unseat her. Thutmose now diligently effaced Hatshepsut's name wherever it appeared on her monuments, just as Hatshepsut had effaced the name of her servant Senmut. It was standard Egyptian practice to try to obliterate the name of a discredited predecessor from history, but the practice did not always achieve its aim. Like pencil erasures, the chiseled effacements often left the original inscriptions discernible.

Once at the helm, Thutmose spun the ship of state about and put it back on the course his grandfather had taken—foreign conquest. In the south, to be sure, Hatshepsut's predecessors had made an excellent start; Thutmose had little to do there. His great achievement lay in consolidating and making permanent what his grandfather had begun, the conquest and annexation of Palestine and Syria. It took 15 or more campaigns before Thutmose was satisfied that he had the area properly subdued.

He reached his high-water mark during his eighth campaign, when he went beyond the Euphrates to fight the Mitanni empire, which had clashed with his grandfather. The preparations he undertook would indicate that one of the secrets of Thutmose's success was a genius for careful planning. For this operation he ordered boats to be loaded on oxcarts and hauled more than 250 miles to be used as transports for ferrying his men across the river. By the time of Thutmose's death, the Egyptian empire stretched from Syria to what is now the Sudan.

The word "empire" as applied to Egypt needs defining. The closest Egypt came to organized rule was in Nubia, where a viceroy was in charge of the whole area, with an armed force and administrative staff at his command, and where the pharaohs built forts and temples and founded towns. The Nubians as a result eventually became Egyptianized. Egypt's rule in Palestine and Syria, on the other hand, was far looser; protectorate might be a better term to describe it than empire. The basic administration was almost entirely in the hands of the native princes. These men were watched over by an Egyptian high commissioner in residence at Gaza who had subordinates spotted in important towns. Mil-

itary force was limited to small and scattered garrisons. What made the system work was the local rulers' awareness of Egypt's iron fist and the swiftness with which it could strike.

There were other ways of keeping the empire together besides the threat of force. For one, there was the practice of carrying off to Egypt the sons or brothers of Syrian and Palestinian princes as hostages. This practice paid additional dividends: the youths, often brought up from an early age in an Egyptian environment, returned to their fatherlands with warm and deep-seated feelings for their foster home.

Once Egypt had embarked on this adventure into building an empire, there was no turning back. On the one side the need for security against a recurrence of foreign invasion, and on the other the hard facts of economic involvement (the tribute from dependent states, and the imports of gold and cedar to which Egypt had now become accustomed), guaranteed the perpetuation of the new state of affairs.

And empire transformed the country utterly; it released forces that remade Egyptian society, religion and politics. The nation that had once gloried in isolation was now committed to daily intercourse with foreigners; the nation whose ideals had once been security and stability was now committed to unending insecurity and change. Once upon a time the god-king had been elevated, aloof and circumscribed by ceremonial; now he was accessible to more people but personally attended by fewer. The theory of his divinity remained, but now he was seen to be a fallible and mortal human being. Once the nobles had held such titles as Chief of the Royal Hairdressers and Chief of the Royal Manicurists, and they had performed the services those titles suggest; now most of the titles disappeared, and the few that remained—such as Keeper of the Royal Diadem—were titles of honor indicating no personal service to the king.

THE EMPIRE AT ITS HEIGHT

THE GREATEST LAND AREA *Egypt ever ruled was consolidated as an empire in about 1450 B.C. by the New Kingdom Pharaoh Thutmose III. Encompassing almost 400,000 square miles, it stretched from the Euphrates in the north to the desert beyond Napata in* the south. *Even at the height of the empire, however, the pharaohs had direct control over only the Nile River Valley itself; the more distant lands, especially on the eastern Mediterranean, were simply spheres of influence administered by local princes.*

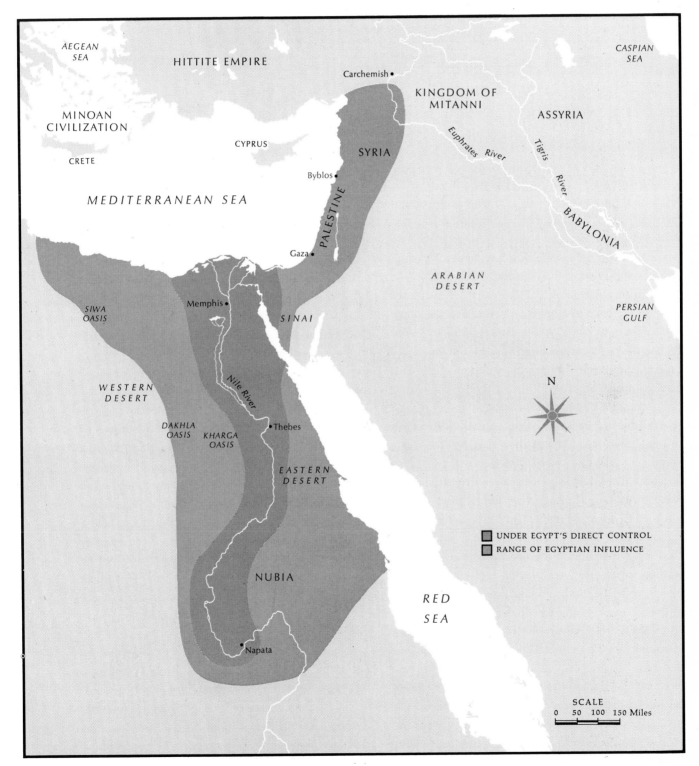

AEGEAN SEA

HITTITE EMPIRE

CASPIAN SEA

Carchemish •

KINGDOM OF MITANNI

ASSYRIA

MINOAN CIVILIZATION

CYPRUS

SYRIA

Euphrates River

Tigris River

CRETE

BABYLONIA

Byblos •

MEDITERRANEAN SEA

PALESTINE

Gaza •

ARABIAN DESERT

PERSIAN GULF

SIWA OASIS

Memphis •

SINAI

WESTERN DESERT

Nile River

N

DAKHLA OASIS   KHARGA OASIS

• Thebes

EASTERN DESERT

■ UNDER EGYPT'S DIRECT CONTROL
■ RANGE OF EGYPTIAN INFLUENCE

NUBIA

RED SEA

• Napata

SCALE
0   50   100   150 Miles

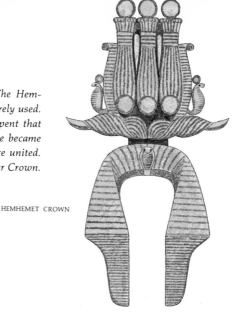

DISTINCTIVE CROWNS *identified Egypt's kings and gods. The Hemhemet Crown of papyrus bundles and sun disks was only rarely used. More familiar were Upper Egypt's White Miter—with a serpent that was a royal emblem—and Lower Egypt's Red Crown. These became one in the pharaoh's Double Crown after the two lands were united. In battle or at military functions the king wore the Blue War Crown.*

HEMHEMET CROWN

WHITE CROWN

With conquest came the responsibility of rule, and this brought in its wake the expansion of bureaucracy and the growth of a professional army. With conquest also came wealth—but the gods to whom the triumphs were due had to receive their share. Temples and temple holdings therefore waxed rich and important. So did the clergy that tended them—a fact that would prove a threat to the pharaoh in years to come. Art, craftsmanship, styles of dress and speech experienced foreign influence. All aspects of life felt the impact of Egypt's transformation into an empire.

Thutmose III administered so well that the machinery he set in motion ran successfully for a full century after him. In the reign of his great-grandson, Amenhotep III, in the 14th Century B.C., the 18th Dynasty reached its zenith. Egypt was at peace and trade was flourishing. Except for putting down a rebellion in Nubia, Amenhotep engaged in few military ventures. He entered instead on a vast building program—a court, colossal statues, a funerary temple for himself and temples in other cities throughout the land.

Then came his son, Amenhotep IV, and with his reign the 18th Dynasty began to falter and the kingdom to shrink. Some indication of the events that were taking place at the outposts of the empire may be found in a collection of clay tablets discovered in the ruins of Tell el Amarna. For a while the tablets were an enigma, for they were inscribed in cuneiform, not hieroglyphics. What

was such a script as this doing among Egyptian remains? But Babylonian cuneiform, like French in the 19th Century, was the diplomatic medium of the ancient world, and study soon revealed that the tablets came from the files of the Pharaoh's foreign office. They consist of letters addressed to the Pharaoh's court, some of them from friendly foreign kings and others from Egyptian vassals, apprising the Pharaoh of threats from enemy foreigners and imploring military assistance. They generally protest that no help has been forthcoming, though sometimes they contradict themselves.

The protests led a generation of scholars to believe that indifference on the part of Amenhotep III and his son and their failure to give help when it was needed allowed the Egyptian empire to fall apart, but that theory is now in dispute. Whether the pharaohs actually ignored the pleas or whether they sent as much help as they deemed necessary, the fact that is that toward the end of the reign of Amenhotep III trouble was brewing aboard. During the reign of his son, Amenhotep IV, the Hittites in Asia Minor, whose star was in the ascendant in this era, pressed forward to take Syria. The Egyptians withdrew some of their garrisons in Palestine and slackened their hold on that land. This was the situation that prevailed when Amenhotep IV began to devote his attention to a subject closer to his heart, a social reform in the guise of a religious reformation.

Amenhotep IV may have been a religious fanatic; certainly he was an ascetic. He was a phys-

RED CROWN   DOUBLE CROWN   WAR CROWN

ically weak man with a long, thin face, drooping shoulders, broad hips and spindly legs. He was also a visionary who was not in tune with his times. He absorbed himself single-mindedly in transforming Egypt internally and hardly glanced at what was happening outside the borders. He engaged in a life-and-death struggle with the bureaucracy and the clergy, which had become well-entrenched, and powerful blocs since the time of Thutmose III, and were now cramping the Pharaoh's authority. He mustered an administrative establishment of his own choosing, drawing heavily on the army for personnel, and installed it in a new capital that he built at a site in the middle of Egypt about 200 miles south of what is now Cairo, near the modern site of Tell el Amarna.

Amenhotep IV was determined to restore the kingship to the exalted position it had had in the days of the Old Kingdom. To do that he had to displace the clergy, and to displace the clergy he had to destroy the gods the clergy served. At Tell el Amarna, far from Thebes, he undertook to revolutionize Egypt's religion. He tried to overthrow the polytheistic accretion of centuries and in particular to replace the traditional worship of the god Amon with the worship of Aton, conceived as a single, universal god, the source of all life, and represented by the sun's disk. He changed his name from Amenhotep, which meant "Amon is content, the god ruler of Thebes," to Akhenaton, "Serviceable-to-the-Aton"—the name by which he is known

to history. He called his new capital Akhetaton, "the Horizon of Aton." With the frenzy of a fanatic, he directed his agents to remove the name and image of Amon from all temples and tombs, and in some places to remove the phrase "the gods."

But Akhenaton did not allow the people direct access to the god; he and his family worshiped Aton, and the people were meant to worship him, the god-king. His revolution failed. Within a decade, Akhenaton was dead and the Egyptians returned to their old ways. The chisel-wielders reappeared to hack out Akhenaton's name as assiduously as they had earlier removed Amon's. The government was returned to Thebes, and Akhetaton fell into ruins that slept undisturbed until the arrival of the 19th Century Egyptologists.

It was the army that had enabled Akhenaton to break with tradition, and it was the army that returned Egypt to tradition. The army made peace with the civil service and with the clergy, and all of these institutions shared power. In the new age that now opened, the throne paid careful attention to the rights and prerogatives of all three. The rulers were the pharaohs of the 19th and 20th Dynasties, the first of whom began his career as an army commander and 11 of whom bore the celebrated name Ramses.

The period spanned by these two dynasties presents a curious contradiction. On the one hand, it was perhaps Egypt's showiest age. The pharaohs won victories over foreign enemies, erected monumental buildings and presided over a luxurious court. Yet it was also the age that portended Egypt's political disintegration and end as a major power.

In some part this was brought about by forces over which the pharaohs had no control. Great movements were taking place in these times; the stage was being set for a new act in the drama of ancient history. The Near Eastern peoples who had in recent years been clashing with Egypt were making their final appearance; other men, actors in the opening scenes of the great age of Greece, were making their entrance. A great migratory movement from the north and west was just beginning, involving certain peoples new to history: the Tursha or Tyrshenoi, who may have been Etruscans; the Shekresh or Shekelesh or Sikeloi, who may have been Sicilians; the Danuna, who were probably the Danaoi of the *Iliad*; the Sherden, pirates who were later Sardinians; the Peleset, or Philistines, who gave their name to Palestine. The Egyptians, ignorant of the intruders' origins and aware only that they came from across the Mediterranean, referred to them vaguely as the "Sea Peoples." They inundated Egypt's shores, and Egypt expended much energy trying to stem the tide.

Then Egypt's aggressiveness diminished. At the beginning of the 19th Dynasty a pharaoh could still lead an army into Syria; at the end he was desperately defending the homeland and depending largely on foreign troops to do it. Egyptian self-confidence waned. The appearance of the troublesome Sea Peoples, the vicissitudes of the empire and the disruptive effects of Akhenaton's revolution sapped the nation's vigor.

But only the historian, looking down the centuries, can discern all this. At the beginning of the 13th Century B.C., when Ramses II took the throne to open a reign that would last 67 lustrous years, no shadows of decline were visible. Ramses was truly a king of kings. He entered into diplo-

matic negotiations with the Hittites, with whom he signed one of the first recorded treaties in history. He campaigned in Syria and Palestine and raided into the south. His military fame, however, is largely based on his own boastful words. His accounts of his valorous exploits and personal courage survive on the walls of almost every major temple of his era; they show him performing like an Egyptian superman. The size and the number of his monuments are equal to those of the age of the pyramids. Some were begun by his father and completed or added to by Ramses; others were constructions of his own conceiving. Among them are the Great Hypostyle Hall, a ceremonial temple at Karnak; the Ramesseum, the funerary temple he built for the glory of himself and the god Amon on the west bank of the Nile at Thebes; the great temple at Abydos, which he dedicated to the god Osiris; several structures at Memphis, which have since been pillaged; and Abu Simbel, the temple in Nubia with four colossal statues of Ramses facing the river, which have had to be moved from their original site to spare their being inundated by the new High Dam near Aswan.

The age of Ramses, with its great temples, its colossal statues, its glowing accounts of the leader's exploits, marks the climax of the age of the pharaohs. It was an age that had begun with the unification of scattered tribes along a segment of the river and ended with a glorious and far-flung empire that extended well beyond it; an age that began with the fashioning of simple shelter out of the river's mud and ended with the erection of giant monuments out of the neighboring cliffs. It was an age that spanned several millennia, throughout which the pharaoh and his subjects, despite vicissitudes in fortune, were borne on a faith in themselves, in their superiority over other nations, and in the pantheon of which the pharaoh was a member.

A KINGLY THRUST *by Pharaoh Ramses III dispatches a Libyan. Ramses turned back three invasions.*

THE WAR MACHINE

Egyptian documents testify that when war came, officers of the pharaohs' army could mobilize "the entire land" for battle. Scribes had records of the soldiers, the priests, the artisans, the sources of food supply. Conscription agents went into the countryside and rounded up draftees. Reserves were called to duty. In addition, the toughly disciplined troops of Egypt's standing army were ready to fight on land or sea. When a pharaoh ordered, "Bring forth equipment," armories issued spears, bows and shields to the troops. The war machine cut across all social lines. Common field hands, youths with social connections and the pharaoh himself went to the front. In times of trouble, ancient Egypt waged total war.

CLOSE-RANKED EGYPTIANS *bearing long spears march out to meet the enemy. Strictly disciplined, they could be maneuvered in corps of 5,000 men.*

ENEMY WARRIORS, *gripping sword and shield, and wearing body armor, are caught in a thick barrage of long-shafted Egyptian arrows.*

THE HARD LOT OF THE INFANTRY

"Come, I will speak to you of the ills of the infantryman," one ancient scribe wrote. "He is awakened while there is still an hour for sleeping. He is driven like a jackass and he works until the sun sets beneath its darkness of night. He hungers and his belly aches. He is dead while he lives." But, frightened and "calling to his god, 'come to me that you may rescue me,'" he fought. He fought with maces, daggers and spears on fields filled with charging chariots and bronze-tipped arrows.

Between battles a soldier ate well enough. But in times of action, it was said, "his food is the grass of the field like any other head of cattle."

Soldiers were trained from boyhood, "being imprisoned in the barracks" and "pummeled with beatings." Later, they could live with their families between campaigns. Others were foreigners serving as mercenaries or forced into the army after being captured. In 1190 B.C., when the migrating Sea Peoples (including the Sherden shown above) attacked Egypt, the Egyptian army was itself augmented by companies of Sherden mercenaries.

Youths of the upper classes usually enlisted in the separately organized chariot corps. Some of them bought their own chariots and then drove home to show off their driving skill before battle.

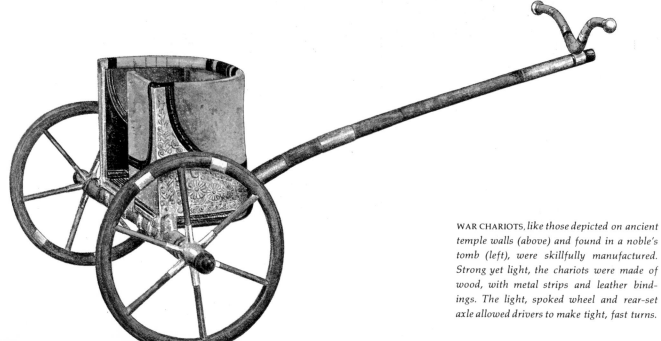

WAR CHARIOTS, *like those depicted on ancient temple walls (above) and found in a noble's tomb (left), were skillfully manufactured. Strong yet light, the chariots were made of wood, with metal strips and leather bindings. The light, spoked wheel and rear-set axle allowed drivers to make tight, fast turns.*

A DEADLY ARSENAL

The principal weapon in the Egyptian arsenal was the bow and arrow. Detachments of archers deftly fought on foot, aided by others in speeding chariots. These two-man vehicles, pulled by horses that Ramses III said "quivered in all their limbs, prepared to crush the foreign countries under their hoofs," crossed the enemy front and raked it with fire, thus softening up the opposing formations. In their wake, Egyptian infantrymen then finished off the broken enemy ranks with hand weapons.

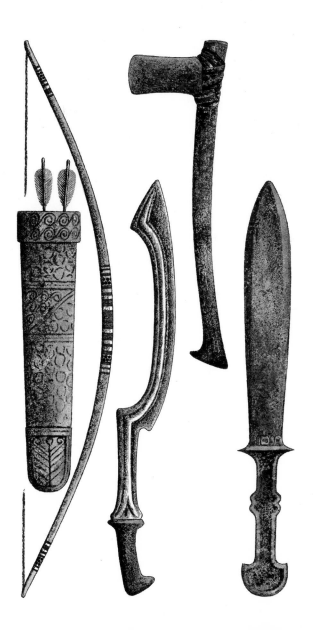

AN EGYPTIAN ARCHER (above) used a bow of wood and animal horn strung with sinew and carried a quiver with 20 to 30 arrows. Other warriors were armed with an assortment of weapons. Shown on this page, besides the standard bow and quiver are, left to right: a scimitar with curved cutting edge; an ax, used by the infantry; and a bronze dagger, used in close combat.

SEAGOING ARCHERS *shoot from an Egyptian warship while enemies fall into the sea. Like all seaborne troops, oarsmen, their heads barely visible, could be identified on land by a leather patch on the seat of their kilts.*

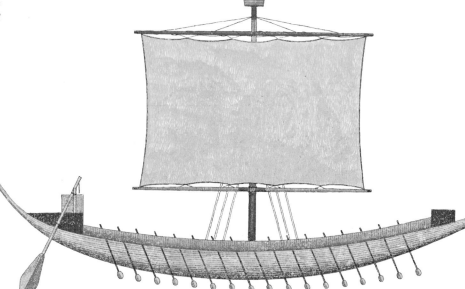

AN EGYPTIAN WARSHIP *(right), steered by a large bladed oar in the stern, usually had a wooden hull, cloth sail and rigging of papyrus fiber. Depending on the ship's size, the crew might number as many as 250 soldiers.*

REPELLING AN INVASION BY SEA

Egypt had no separate navy, but its army was well prepared to fight at sea, as it decisively demonstrated in 1190 B.C. Ramses III tells how, threatened by an armada of Mediterranean seafarers, he set up a defense "like a strong wall, with warships, galleys and skiffs. They were completely equipped both fore and aft with brave fighters carrying their weapons and infantry of all the pick of Egypt."

The Egyptians had two decisive advantages in this famed battle, fought near the mouth of the Nile. First, their firepower was superior to the invading Sea Peoples'. The invaders had only swords and spears and were badly outranged by the Egyptians' arrows. Second, the ships of the Sea Peoples were powered only by sails, while the Egyptian ships were powered by both sails and oars and thus had greater maneuverability. The battle was decided when the invading ships, trapped between Egyptian sea forces and archers on the nearby shore, were "capsized and overwhelmed in their places."

CAPTIVE SOLDIERS *were, in Ramses' words, "pinioned like birds."*
Afterward, the captives were conscripted into the Egyptian army.

THE VICTORS' TALLY
OF THE SPOILS

On the walls of the Medinet Habu temple, Ramses
III depicted what became of the enemies of Egypt
so that it might be "a lesson for a million generations." Men not "overthrown in their blood and
made into heaps," he boasted, were captured with
their women, children and cattle. Their leaders
were "branded and made into slaves stamped with
my name, their women and children treated likewise." Meticulous bookkeepers, the Egyptians kept
a careful tally of every goat, sheep and cow taken
in battle and severed one hand of each slain enemy
so that an exact count could be made. Then the
spoils were dedicated to the national god Amon.

VICTORIOUS EGYPTIANS *bring spoils to the King, the large figure shown at*

left, after a great battle with the Libyans. So many cattle were seized that Ramses was able, he said, to donate "everlasting herds" to Amon's temple.

4
GODS AND THE AFTERLIFE

Western man places religion in a compartment of its own, separating it from other aspects of his existence. To an Egyptian this would have been unthinkable. Religion permeated his whole life—socially, politically and economically. As he saw it, every detail of his own life and of the life around him—from the predictable flooding of the Nile to the chance death of a cat—depended entirely on the attitude of the gods. The New Testament injunction "Render to Caesar the things that are Caesar's and to God the things that are God's" would have meant nothing to him. His Caesar was the pharaoh, and the pharaoh was a god.

The roots of Egyptian religion go far back into primeval times, before there was a pharaoh. Prehistoric Egyptians, like most early peoples, were reverential toward the wonders of nature and the fearsome or admirable traits of animals—the ferocity of the lion, the strength of the crocodile, the tender care of a cow for her young. The first divinities to arise—and divinities continued to rise throughout Egyptian history—were frequently represented in animal form, though they dealt with or oversaw human occupations.

Khnum, one of the gods associated with Creation, was portrayed as a ram, an animal the Egyptians considered unusually prolific. Anubis, the faithful guardian of tombs and a god of the dead, was represented as a recumbent jackal—paradoxically, for the jackal was known to dig up human bones, and indeed the earliest graves were covered with stones not only to mark them for posterity but to keep them safe from marauding jackals. Thoth, the god of learning and wisdom, the inventor of writing, the vizier and official scribe of the afterworld, was alternately symbolized as an ibis and as a baboon, perhaps because the grave facial expressions of these creatures suggested thoughtfulness.

During much of Egyptian history, live animals associated with gods were maintained in the temples, where they dwelt in pampered luxury. A crocodile representing a god of sun, earth and water lolled in the temple pool at Crocodilopolis; the ibis of Thoth was kept at Hermopolis; a cat representing a goddess of joy and love lazed in a temple at Bast; Apis, a sacred bull, was maintained at

A FALCON-HEADED GOD, *Horus appears twice on the temple of Ramses II. Throughout Egypt's history this god was personally identified with the king; each succeeding pharaoh used the name Horus as the first of his titles.*

Memphis. These animals were mummified like human beings when they died.

Besides animals, the Egyptians were in awe of the manifestations of nature. Among their manifold objects of worship, one had eminent qualifications for reverence—the sun. Probably the Egyptians perceived that life was dependent upon the sun, and they worshiped it by various names and in various cults. One of these names was Re. The center of the cult of Re was at Heliopolis (a name given the town by the Greeks and meaning "City of the Sun"). Re was among the first of the gods to achieve nationwide recognition, and throughout Egyptian history he remained one of the most important deities in the land.

The worship of animals and nature is common to early societies, when man is dominated by the world around him and exists at its mercy. As he grows in sophistication, as he learns to come to grips with nature, as his awe of its mysteries diminishes and his appreciation of his own talents awakens, then his gods undergo a transition from zoomorphic to anthropomorphic concepts. So it was with the Egyptians. Sometime before the rise of the First Dynasty, anthropomorphism, the conception of gods in human form, made its appearance in Egyptian religion.

But tradition does not die easily, and old religious concepts are not replaced at one stroke. The Egyptians adopted anthropomorphism gradually, fusing the three ideas of nature, animal and man. One of the earliest deities to undergo this fusion was Hathor, the goddess of love and childbirth; she was given a human body and head but retained an element of her animal manifestation—a pair of cow's horns. Another was Thoth, who acquired a human body but kept the head of the ibis. Still later Anubis—who came to play a role as judge of the dead as well as guardian of the tombs—took on a human body but kept his jackal's head. Khnum

assumed a human body but retained the head of a ram; and when he did, the myth surrounding his role in Creation had him fashioning men (and every baby still to be born) on a potter's wheel.

Gods that arose later than these were portrayed in fully human form from the time of their inception. One of the earliest was Ptah, the god of craftsmen, who first appeared in history when Memphis was founded as the capital of the Old Kingdom; it was at this time that society was organized and crafts became an important part of the social organization. Another was Osiris, the ruler of the netherworld, who was always portrayed as a dead man.

Osiris was a god-king—perhaps a legendary outgrowth of a real ruler, perhaps a primitive god of fertility—who was believed to have given Egypt civilization. He had an evil brother, Seth, who was jealous of the devotion of his brother's subjects and slew Osiris. At length the slain King was resurrected through the perseverance of his wife, Isis, who roamed the earth in search of the dismembered parts of his body until she collected them all. Their son, Horus, later avenged his father's murder by vanquishing Seth and winning from him the rule of the earth. According to the myth, every pharaoh ruled on earth as Horus. When he died he became Osiris and ruled the underworld. His son, the new Pharaoh, took up the rule on earth as Horus.

These are only a few of the multiple deities and overlapping personalities that populated Egyptian religion. From the beginning of their religious life to the end, the Egyptians had an abundance of gods. This was because their land always consisted basically of a conglomeration of small agricultural communities. Each locality claimed its own particular deity, and when the communities were united under the pharaohs they did not discard the local deities. Instead they united the various gods, identifying one with another and joining some of them into families. The prominence of a god and the

MUMMIFIED ANIMALS *associated with the gods were often placed in tombs in New Kingdom and Ptolemaic times. A cat (left) and a crocodile mummy mask (below) were identified respectively with Bastet, a delta goddess, and Sobek, god of a city called Crocodilopolis.*

union he might make were coincident with the political and economic fortune of the town of his origin. Gods of old villages combined with those of communities rising into prominence; gods of places on the rise were united with well-established deities.

For example, the god of Memphis was Ptah. At the beginning of the dynastic era, when Memphis was founded by the Pharaoh Menes as the capital of the united land, Ptah became the patron of royalty. As the influence of Memphis spread, Ptah was wedded to the lion goddess Sekhmet, who presided in a nearby territory. But Menes' personal god was Horus, the falcon, or sky god, who could sweep through the heavens and survey the united domain; and so Horus and the pharaoh came to be one.

Similarly, by the time of the Fourth Dynasty, when Heliopolis had grown in influence and the cult of the sun god Re emanated from there, the pharaoh became the son of Re.

One god that did not arise until Egyptian civilization was well under way illustrates perhaps better than any of the others how the fortune of a god depended upon the place of his origin. This was Amon of Thebes. Both the town and the god were obscure prior to the founding of the Middle Kingdom. But Thebes was where the Middle Kingdom rulers arose; the pharaohs credited the local god with the reunification of Egypt; and the city remained important throughout Egyptian history, even when the capital was moved elsewhere.

The name "Amon" meant "hidden"; the god was an invisible being—sometimes conceived as the breath that animates all living things—and hence he was a spirit that might be everywhere present. Thus that spirit spread throughout the land, aided by the influence of the Theban rule.

Even a spirit needs portrayal by a people given to pictorial expression, and so the god Amon received a physical representation. He was shown in many different ways: sometimes as a ram, a goose or a primeval serpent (creatures that may at some prehistoric time have been associated with a prototype of Amon), but most frequently as a crowned king. When he was shown as a king, the crown often carried a pair of feathers symbolizing the two lands of Upper and Lower Egypt, or the twisted horns of a ram; and when Amon was eventually merged with the sun god Re, the crown showed the rays of the sun. Sometimes it combined all of these emblems.

By the time that Egypt had grown to an empire, the image of Amon accompanied the march of the Egyptian army through the ancient world. In the course of Egyptian history the most massive temple of all time was erected in his honor—the temple complex at Karnak, which is in the neighborhood of Thebes.

Amon not only guided imperial fighting expeditions; he also oversaw the exploitation of the mines in Nubia and Sudan—taking as his due a share of the yield. The worship of Amon extended even beyond Egypt; he became the god of Nubia and for a time he was worshiped in Syria and Palestine. It was said that his rays reached the ends of the earth.

All the combining of gods still left Egypt basically a land of local deities. Each god was usually conceived as being immanent to his place of origin, and there he dwelt in a temple erected specifically for him. His worship, however, was not necessarily rooted for all time in the locality of his conception. Without suppressing reverence to other deities, a god could soar in popularity, become supreme in the nation, and remain so for as long as the city or the men that worshiped him remained influential. The worship of that god then spread in varying degrees across the land, and small sanctuaries appeared in towns and villages as branches of his principal shrine. As a supreme god, he became incarnate in the pharaoh, so the pharaoh was many gods in one; he was Ptah, the son of Ptah and the

son of Re at the same time that he was Horus and the son of Osiris.

The Egyptians entertained not only a multiplicity of gods but several alternative mythological accounts to explain the same phenomenon. Each important religious center (that is, each important city where a god was worshiped) had its own version of Creation. The priests of Heliopolis attributed Creation to Atum, a god pictured as a human being but identified with the sun god Re. Their theory had to do with the appearance of light in the darkness. The founders of the Middle Kingdom at Thebes ascribed Creation to Amon.

The people of Memphis had a remarkable theory. They posed the question: What caused the act of Creation? As Greek philosophers would later do, the priests of Memphis sought for a First Principle, and they arrived at the theory that Ptah, the god of Memphis, had created the world by acts of his heart and tongue. To the Egyptians "heart and tongue" meant "mind and speech"; they were saying that Ptah conceived the idea of the universe, and that he executed that idea by uttering a command. In other words, they were postulating that there was an articulate intelligence and will behind Creation. This was a profound thought that has no parallel at this early period of man's history.

Most Egyptians, whatever god they worshiped, envisioned the birth of the world as the rising of an earthen mound out of the chaos of primordial waters—an image no doubt suggested by the annual emergence of high points of land out of the receding Nile flood. The priests of Memphis, Heliopolis, Hermopolis and Thebes all claimed their respective cities as the site of this primordial hill.

Religions have ethical content as well as objects of worship, and the Egyptians' chief ethic was one called *maat*. The word is almost impossible to translate precisely, but it involved a combination of such ideas as "order," "truth," "justice" and "righteous-

FOLK GODS, *Sekhmet, Bes and Thoueris (left to right) were among the multitude of deities that commanded local followings. These gods were often associated with animals and their presumed powers; they existed alongside the panoply of major Egyptian deities. War goddess Sekhmet—part woman, part lioness—caused and cured epidemics; Bes, a lion-headed dwarf, scared off evil spirits; Thoueris, a hippopotamus, ensured fertility and safe childbirth.*

SEKHMET BES THOUERIS

ness." *Maat* was considered a quality not of men but of the world, built into it by the gods at the moment of Creation. As such, it represented the gods' will. A person endeavored to act in accordance with the divine will because that was the only way to place himself in harmony with the gods. For the Egyptian peasant *maat* meant working hard and honestly; for the official it meant dealing justly.

During the bitter troubles and disillusionment that beset the First Intermediate Period, the idea briefly emerged that *maat* was not just a passive quality inherent in the world, but that the god-king's subjects had a right to expect its exercise. This was a step toward the development of a concept of social justice, but it did not long survive. Once the Middle Kingdom restored Egypt to prosperity, life was easygoing again and people forgot to worry about how *maat* was to be maintained.

Conceived as a quality passively inherent in the nature of the world, *maat* had limitations. Because

it was the handiwork of the gods and not of men's consciences, it was expected to maintain the god-given and changeless perfection of the world and of society. Thus it precluded any serious questioning of the structure of society or any possibility of reforming it. The world and everything in it had been created by the gods precisely in the form they wanted. Everything therefore was just as it should be—fixed, eternal and proper. War, pestilence and drought were mere temporary upsets of the established cosmic order. Since the world had been as it should be from the moment of Creation, there could not by definition have been a previous, better age, nor would there be a better age to come. Egyptian mythology had no Garden of Eden, no bygone Golden Age, no Armageddon.

The same attitude determined the Egyptians' conception of and emphasis on death. Their beliefs concerning afterlife, like those concerning their gods, had ancient roots in the Nile Valley. Tombs of the Neolithic Age reveal tools and food left with the dead, objects that could only have been intended for use by the departed. The Egyptians envisioned the hereafter as a duplication of the best moments of earthly existence. There was nothing morbid in their lifelong preoccupation with death; they prepared for it earnestly and confidently.

Up to his final moment, every Egyptian of means busied himself with the preparation of a tomb in which to spend eternity and the articles with which to furnish it. In the case of a pharaoh or noble, a tomb might take years or even decades to make ready. He ordered artisans to portray on its walls or in wooden models the activities he expected to carry on—sailing, hunting, fowling, banqueting—as well as tasks to be performed by his servants—weaving, baking, herding, tilling.

In the First Intermediate Period, when nobles were impoverished and men of undistinguished birth rose in the world, the belief emerged that even a high station in life would not exempt one from menial work after death; and from the Middle Kingdom on, tombs were plentifully supplied with articles called *ushebtis.* These were figurines that were expected to answer in place of the deceased when the gods called for labor to tend the celestial fields, in order that the deceased could spend his time in leisure. Once they began to appear, the number of *ushebtis* placed in a tomb steadily increased. Many tombs had hundreds, and some had thousands.

Just as there were many gods and many ideas of Creation, so there were alternative views of the afterlife. The solar cult held that the dead pharaoh boarded the sun's heavenly boat and accompanied him on his daily sail across the firmament above the world by day and through the sky beneath at night. (The world was thought to be a cube bounded on four sides by high mountains on which the sky rested. There was another sky beneath the earth.) The cult of Osiris, on the other hand, held that the pharaoh passed into the underworld to become Osiris and rule below as he had on earth. Because of the Egyptians' consuming concern for their future after death, Osiris came to be universally their mortuary god, one of their most important deities, and less susceptible to alteration than the gods concerned with life.

In the beginning, the denial of death was limited to the pharaoh and his family; only they were divine and immortal. By the time the Old Kingdom was ended, the belief had widened to include nobles; they might, with royal permission, set their tombs close to the pharaoh's and inscribe on the walls of their own tombs their services to him. They hoped thus to share immortality through proximity. Servants and other menials whose functions might be useful to their departed masters perhaps attained a modicum of eternal bliss by being depicted or mentioned in the tombs of the mighty.

With the upheaval that occurred in the First Intermediate Period and the shifting of social classes that resulted, there came a democratization of the Osirian cult. Mortals of ordinary parentage might now share in the blessings of the afterlife, just as they were obviously sharing in the fine things of the present world. Conversely, good parentage was no guarantee of continued good life. Magic formulas—prayers that were previously the prerogative of the pharaoh—were now available to anyone who could pay a priest to intone them at burial or an artisan to inscribe them on coffin walls or papyrus rolls. Properly executed, they enabled anyone who could afford them to join the immortal gods after death and become an Osiris. The term "Osiris" entered the vernacular to designate any deceased person; the phrase "Osiris Ahmose" meant in effect "the late John Doe."

To the Egyptian, the afterlife meant a corporeal existence, not a ghostly substitute. The soul left the body at death, but it was expected to be able

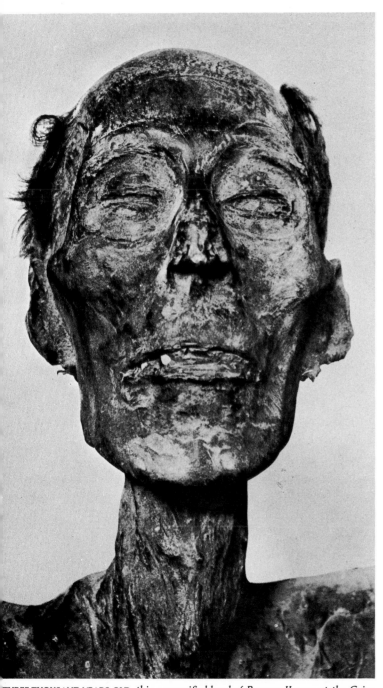

THREE THOUSAND YEARS OLD, *this mummified head of Ramses II now at the Cairo Museum attests to the ancient embalmer's skill. When archeologists discovered and unwrapped the mummy in 1881, its dried skin, teeth and hair were still intact. Having survived the centuries, the mummy suffered a singular indignity on the way to Cairo: a befuddled Egyptian inspector taxed it as imported dried fish.*

to return to it throughout eternity. That was why the Egyptians mummified their dead—to preserve their bodies from decay.

No Egyptian accounts exist to describe mummification. Current knowledge of the process is based largely on writings of Herodotus and on examinations of mummies themselves. The practice varied in detail at different times, but in theory it was a re-enactment of the ministrations the god Osiris was believed to have been given for his resurrection, and the priests who mummified the dead acted the roles of Anubis and the other gods who had restored Osiris.

After the mummy was prepared, it was entombed with articles that the deceased was expected to want or need in his new life—food, sandals, jewels, and a crown or scepter if he was a pharaoh. The custom of leaving food was never entirely abandoned, but in some places amulets (miniature stone or faïence models of sandals, scepters and cuts of meat) came to be substituted for the real articles.

Few Egyptians, of course, could afford so elaborate a burial as this. A pauper could expect little more than a coarse cloth wrapping to serve as a coffin, and burial in a communal grave that was covered with sand. Even the poorest Egyptian burials, however, show some attempt to equip the deceased for the afterlife, though the equipment might consist of no more than a few scraps of food and possibly some crude utensils.

A well-stocked tomb made up the greater part of an Egyptian's preparation for death, but not the whole. He also arranged for periodic observances of certain funerary rites. These were held daily if he was rich, and at the time of festivals if he was of modest means. The rites consisted mainly of offerings of food. Many other ancient peoples gave food to their gods or their dead, but they generally burned it as a sacrifice. The Egyptians, being too practical for waste, returned to the tomb after a decent interval and ate it themselves.

In the Old Kingdom, the funerary duties fell upon the heirs, but later the practice arose of setting aside a portion of a man's estate (that is, the yield of his land in grain, flax, animals and fowl) to pay special mortuary priests for taking over the tasks. In the case of the pharaohs, these endowments became a serious burden on Egypt's economy, since they diverted important revenues from the state to the temples. They also help explain how the priests eventually acquired sufficient wealth and power to threaten the position of the pharaoh.

Men fondly expected that the tombs and the services would be maintained in perpetuity. Human nature being what it is, however, many graves went neglected after a time. As the generations slipped by, descendants focused their attention more on arrangements for their recent dead than on those for remote ancestors. The endowment funds were not infrequently appropriated by the very priests who were supposed to use them for the tombs and the services. All but a few of the tombs were eventually abandoned and looted.

In one phase of Egyptian religion there was uniformity throughout the land—the daily ritual in the temple. Gods, like the dead, were expected to have the same needs and wishes as human beings—food, cleanliness, rest and entertainment. Just as servants provided for the needs of the living, so priests (who in Egyptian were literally "gods' servants") provided for the needs of the gods.

No matter which god they served, priests everywhere up and down the Valley of the Nile performed an elaborate morning ritual that varied little from the time of the Old Kingdom onward.

Following a purificatory bath at dawn in a sacred pool, a company of about a dozen priests entered the temple gates, filed across an open court and made their way inside the temple proper. The public might watch the procession through the

IN RITUAL GARB *of leopard skin over linen, King Ay, dressed as a high priest, is portrayed on a wall of the tomb of his predecessor, Tutankhamen. In Ay's hand is an adz, a knife-sharp tool used symbolically to open the mummy's mouth and restore the body's vital functions for the afterlife. Physical purity was expected of the priests, particularly during their service in the temples. Taboos were extended to their dress; wool and leather were forbidden, though high priests were allowed to wear the skins of certain animals as outer garments while performing temple rites.*

courtyard but could not go beyond that. Once inside the temple, the highest-ranking priest approached the sanctuary and broke the clay seals on its doors. At the moment when the sun thrust its first rays over the horizon, the priest swung open the doors to reveal the effigy of the god, a mummylike figure that was a little smaller than a man. He prostrated himself before the god, rose and chanted prayers, and purified the air with incense. He removed the image from its niche, divested it of its garments, cleansed it, clothed it in fresh raiment, perfumed it and set it back in place. Finally he presented the god with food and drink. At the close of the ceremony, the priest resealed the sanctuary and departed, carefully erasing his footprints and every other evidence that he had been there.

The daily routine varied at the time of the great festivals when the images of the gods, in full panoply and accompanied by a cortège, left their temples and traveled through the countryside. A festival was considered to be entertainment for the god as well as the people, and it was the only time when the people were allowed in the vicinity of the deities. Now they lined the streets to watch.

There were many festivals, but perhaps the most spectacular was one held during the time of the flood in honor of Amon. In a colorful procession of all the priests, Amon was carried from his shrine at Karnak to the banks of the Nile, where he boarded a sacred barge and was towed upstream to the temple of Luxor. He stayed there for nearly a month and then returned to Karnak with similar pomp. Another celebration rich in pageantry took place at Abydos, which was the site of the tombs of the early pharaohs and believed by many Egyptians to be the place where Osiris' head was buried. The city was the goal of a popular pilgrimage. Every Egyptian who could afford it made a journey there to attend a dramatic re-creation of the Osiris myth.

The priests who conducted the services ranked in descending hierarchy below the pharaoh, whose delegates they were. In theory all accessions to the priesthood were subject to the pharaoh's approval, and it was his pleasure to appoint whomever he wished to religious office. In practice, however, the priesthood was for the most part hereditary, passed on from father to son. On occasion, a vacancy in a temple was filled through election by a committee of the priests themselves. By the time of the New Kingdom, it was not uncommon for a person seeking lifetime security to purchase a priestly office for the sake of its comfortable income.

Only the few priests who were authorized to enter the innermost temple sanctum and assist in the divine toilet devoted full time to the service of the god. Other priests, of lower rank, were specialists—astrologers, scholars, readers of the sacred texts, scribes, singers and musicians—and these served on a rotating basis, forsaking their civil life to live within the temple precincts one month out of every four. Also in rotating attendance were the priests comprising the low clergy—the bearers of sacred objects, interpreters of dreams and overseers of temple artisans.

During their period of service, both specialists and minor priests led a life of monastic purity. They shaved their entire bodies (including their eyebrows and lashes), washed frequently and abstained from relations with women. Like sacerdotal men of all societies, Egyptian priests were distinguishable from other citizens by their dress—a brief white linen cloth around the loins, which from predynastic times never succumbed to changes in fashion. Off duty, both specialists and minor priests lived in the secular world like everyone else.

Women served as part-time priestesses and sometimes performed the same functions as their male counterparts. In one instance during the 18th Dynasty, the pharaoh appointed his queen to one of the most eminent religious offices in the land—that of second high priest to the god Amon at Karnak. In the main, however, priestesses were limited to filling the roles of singers and musicians.

The age of Egypt's empire was marked by changes that affected most of the nation's traditional standards, including those pertaining to religion and to the pharaoh. In the days of the Old Kingdom, the pharaoh had been sole and undisputed source of the divine word. As national gods proliferated—and with them the elaborate apparatus of the priesthood—the pharaoh's divine authority diminished, while the wealth and power of the priests grew. This was the situation that prevailed in the latter half of the 18th Dynasty, when the Pharaoh Akhenaton launched a heretical revolt against the great god Amon, the principal deity of the time, and sought to impose upon Egypt a new god and a new form of worship.

The details of Akhenaton's revolution belong with the history of the pharaohs, for the reform he attempted was as much social as religious, and it had more to do with the person of the king than with the religious spirit of the people. Yet even though Akhenaton did not succeed in establishing the worship of his god, the Aton, or in eradicating the other gods, his attempts to do so marked a turning point in Egyptian religious history. Perhaps in reaction against the monolithic nature of the new creed, perhaps because the people were groping in a direction the Hebrews soon would reach, religious worship after Akhenaton's time became more personal than before.

Prior to his time hymns had described the features of the gods without relating them to human wants; a hymn to the sun god Re, for example, declares, "How beautiful it is when thou arisest on the horizon and lightenest the Two Lands [Upper and Lower Egypt] with thy rays." It goes on for many verses in the same vein.

After Akhenaton the idea of a relationship between man and his gods emerged. A hymn from the reign of Ramses IV in the 12th Century B.C. goes in part as follows: "And thou shalt give me health, life and old age, a long reign, strength to all my limbs. . . . And thou shalt give me to eat . . . and thou shalt give me to drink. . . ." The gods were now seen not only as fashioners of the universe and capricious troublemakers, but as responsible for the welfare of their creatures, compassionate toward human needs and responsive to human pleas.

But not long after this personal spirit emerged, the priesthood and religious ceremony atrophied, and when Egyptian civilization began to decline the worship of animals was revived and intensified. By the time Greek conquerors reached the land of the Nile in the Fourth Century B.C., when the empire had collapsed and the country was beset by economic woes, the people had grown insecure and had lost their enthusiasm for life. Instead of confidence, their religion stressed humility, submissiveness and patience. Death was no longer seen as a continuance of the pleasures of life, but loomed instead as surcease from earthly tribulations.

In its time their religion had served the Egyptians well. By commingling the gods and the pharaoh, and ultimately uniting the people with them, it provided a cohesion that helped their civilization to survive for nearly 3,000 years. In the room it made for new gods and diverse ideas, it allowed the people pliancy. Polytheism may be bewildering in its disparities, but it goes hand in hand with tolerance; and tolerance spared Egypt under the pharaohs much of the discord, cleavage and bloodshed that other peoples have suffered in the name of religion. By its concern for the dead it made the civilization immortal; and in its zeal for conservation it left to posterity the remains of a memorable grandeur.

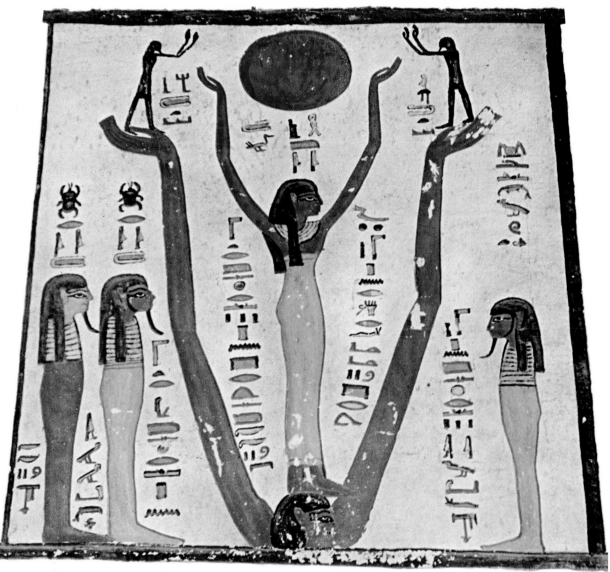

THE MYSTICAL KA, *the immortal spirit said to dwell in every man, is depicted here with arms upraised and a goddess standing on its head.*

THE WORLD OF THE DEAD

At the beginning of the Old Kingdom, only pharaohs were entitled to an afterlife. But by the time of the New Kingdom, 11 centuries later, life after death was the expectation of all Egyptians. They carefully prepared for a hectic hereafter in which, according to one Egyptologist, "The dead man is at one and the same time in heaven, in the god's boat, under the earth, tilling the Elysian fields, and in his tomb enjoying his victuals." For the wealthy, elaborate embalming and well-stocked tombs assured a house for the Ka, or soul, and the Ba, or physical vitality, which fled a body at death. But a dead man still went forth to be judged by Osiris, god of the underworld. Osiris, weighing his virtues and faults, could then mete out either a renewed life in eternity—or a second death of extinction.

A WEEPING WIDOW *crouches at her mummified husband's feet as attending priests start final rituals before burial.*

PREPARATIONS FOR THE AFTERLIFE

In the brief limbo between life and afterlife, the ancient Egyptian was made ready for eternity by a complex funeral liturgy. This centered about the embalming ritual which, according to Herodotus, might take up to 70 days to complete if the deceased was a man of substance (for the poor, a day or two sufficed). Since the dead man's spirits would inhabit his body, the embalmers sought to preserve the mortal remains for eternity. To accomplish this,

they used compounds of salts, spices and resins to preserve and dry the eviscerated corpse into a shriveled mummy, then stuffed and swathed it with layers of finely woven linen. Returned to the bereaved family—whose ranks were often swelled by professional mourners—the mummy underwent the symbolic Opening of the Mouth ceremony shown above. Prepared to eat, drink and speak again, the dead man was at last ready for the tomb.

HIRED MOURNERS, *tears streaming from their eyes, augment a family's sorrow. Such professional weepers were often employed for Egyptian funerals.*

PARADE TO THE TOMB

Egyptian funerary ritual called for burial in the west, where the sun was believed to begin its nightly journey across the underworld. In the bleak western desert stood immense necropolises—cities of the dead—whose pyramids, temples and

rock-cut tombs were built and maintained for those who could afford an affluent afterlife. Great processions of mourners like the ones on these pages brought the encased mummies (not shown here) to these tombs, first by barge across the Nile and then overland by ox-drawn sledge. Led by shaven-headed priests who wafted incense and intoned the ritual chants, the procession ended at the door of the tomb, where the last rites might include a solemn ceremonial dance and a funeral feast.

JUDGMENT IN THE UNDERWORLD

"Do justice whilst thou endurest upon earth," reads an ancient papyrus entitled "The Instruction for King Merikare." "A man remains over after death, and his deeds are placed beside him in heaps. However, existence yonder is for eternity, and . . . for him who reaches it without wrongdoing, he shall exist yonder like a god." The essence of Egyptian mortuary religion was a universal faith in the final judgment of the god Osiris. Usually depicted as a mummy, Osiris stonily supervised the weighing of the dead man's heart while truth occupied the balancing scale. For those who failed this test, a fierce beast called The Devourer of Souls awaited. But most passed, and could look forward to an infinity of the pleasant pursuits they had known in life—the mummy, at home in his tomb, was surrounded by pictures and statuettes of his servants and even his concubines.

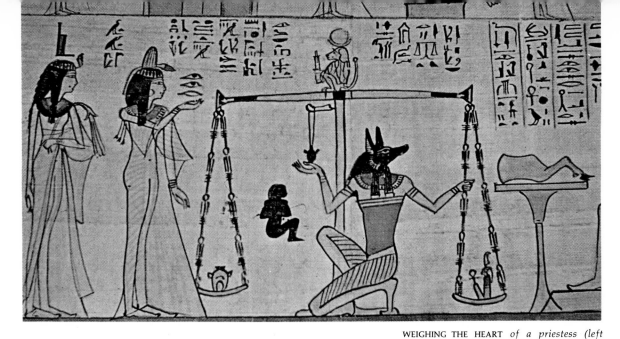

WEIGHING THE HEART *of a priestess (left scale), jackal-headed Anubis balances it against a figure representing truth; baboon-like Thoth, atop the scales, records the result. At right is an offering of a haunch of beef.*

HOMAGE TO OSIRIS *is paid by a nobleman and his wife in a tomb scene probably painted in their lifetime. The offering and hieroglyphic paeans were calculated to assure a warm reception in the underworld.*

BOATS AND BIRDS
FOR JOURNEYS OF THE DEAD

While early Egyptian cults disagreed on what a dead man could and could not do in his afterlife, New Kingdom Egyptians devised an ingenious synthesis of the major beliefs. Thus, a dead man was said to remain in his tomb by day, although he might revisit the living through his wandering spirit, the birdlike Ba *(right)*. At sunset he boarded his solar boat to accompany the sun through the underworld—a journey borrowed from the sun worship of the Old Kingdom. He might stop to work in the magnificent Field of Reeds—a pleasant enough task if he had been a hard-working farmer in life. But at dawn, he returned to his tomb for the food and rest that even the dead required.

A SHIP OF THE DEAD, *in model form, was often left in tombs for travel in the afterworld. The mummy, adorned with the likeness of Osiris, reposes between the figures of Isis and Nephthys, the god's mourning sisters.*

THE WINGED BA, *a spirit symbolizing the physical survival of the dead, was thought to have the ability to leave a tomb. Through the medium of the Ba, a dead man could return to his haunts in the mortal world.*

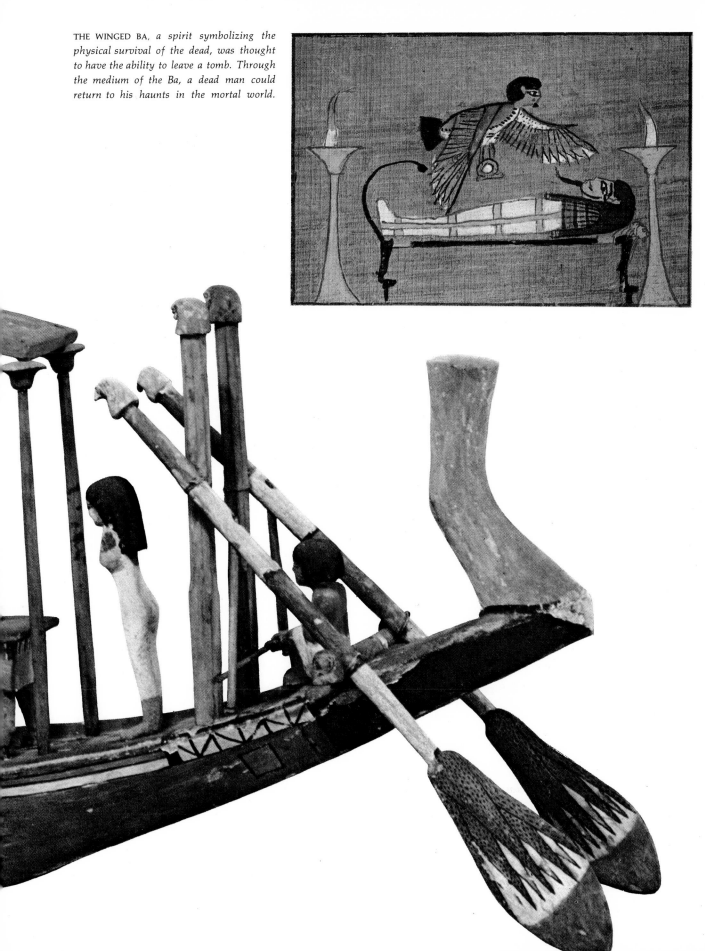

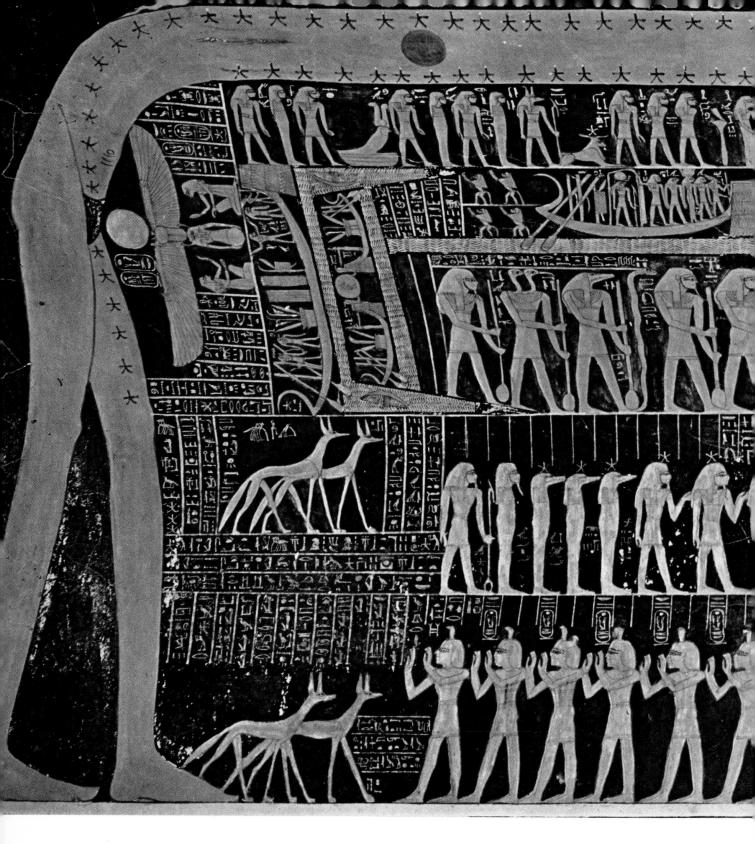

A HEAVENLY HORDE

A special part of the afterworld was reserved for Egypt's bewildering assortment of gods. Under the Old Kingdom, each city had its own set of deities: Re was worshipped at Heliopolis, Amon at Thebes, Ptah at Memphis and Thoth at Hermopolis. But by the New Kingdom, some degree of order had been

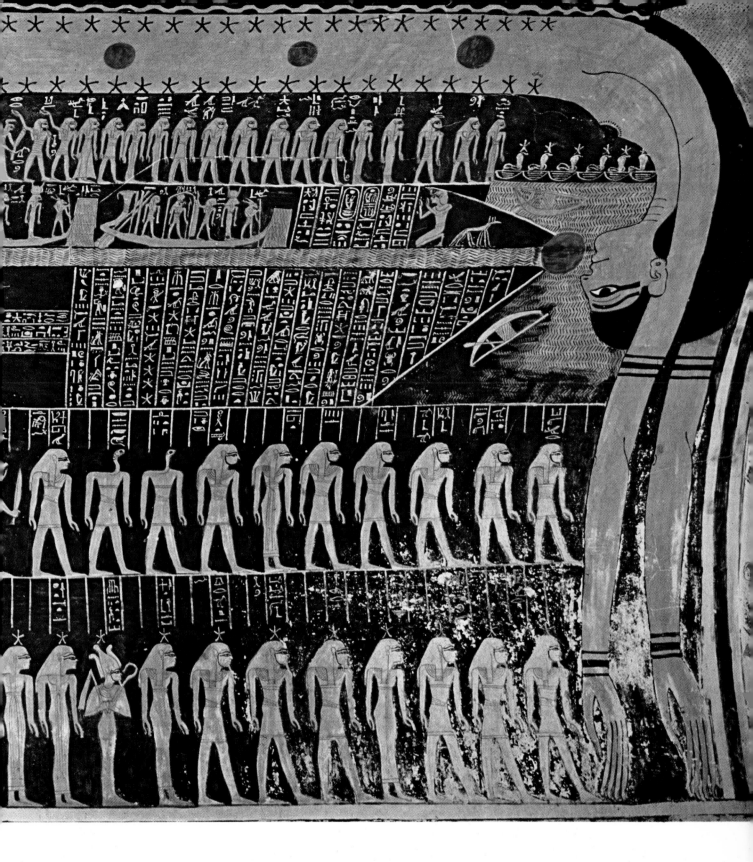

established in the cluttered cosmology by the priesthoods of the major gods. It then became possible to depict a united heavenly family in a group portrait, as in this mural from the tomb of Ramses VI. Framing the universe is the arched body of Nut, the sky goddess, one of the principal cosmic deities.

According to one legend, Nut swallowed the sun each evening (it is shown as a brown disc passing through her star-bordered body) and gave birth to it again in the morning. Arrayed beneath Nut is the host of gods and demigods that the Pharaoh —himself a living god—confidently expected to join in death.

5

THE PHARAOH
AND HIS PEOPLE

Almost every society has been likened in structure to the pyramid. No society better fits the analogy than that of ancient Egypt, the land to which the pyramid is indigenous. At the apex of Egyptian society stood the pharaoh, who was god and king in one. Below him, in descending order and increasing numbers, were nobles, officials, scribes, artisans, unskilled laborers and peasants. The small group at the top of the structure was endowed with wealth and power; a somewhat larger group below it was involved in the administration of the wealth and power; and millions toiled in the workshops and the fields.

The pharaoh was the embodiment of the gods and the soul of the state. He was responsible for the rise and fall of the Nile, the yield of the soil, the health of the commerce, the fortunes of the army and the maintenance of the peace. He owned the land, directed the energies of the people and spoke the law.

A ruler cast in this mold particularly fitted Egypt's requirements, for a king of superhuman authority was necessary to effect and maintain unification in a land that was 750 miles long. The king acquired deputies, of course, to dispense his justice, perform his religious functions, supervise his public works and lead his military expeditions. But as he was a god, he was thought to be everywhere present. The justice and leadership therefore were all his. The officials who represented him were not considered to have power in their own right, but only to voice his commands.

Because all Egyptian life was permeated with religion, there was no distinct church-state separation such as is known in the modern West; where the ruler is god, civil and religious affairs run together. There was, however, a division of responsibilities among the pharaoh's deputies, and the men charged with carrying out his will developed proprietary concerns of their own as the state evolved. Each of the resulting divisions saw an era when its officers shared in the wealth and power of the pharaoh.

The first was civil administration, which was run by the vizier. The second was the administration of temples, which was in the hands of high priests. The third was the professional army, which did

AFTER THE HUNT *a servant dresses geese killed by his master. Hunting was a favorite pastime of wealthy Egyptians, and wild fowl was a prized delicacy. At one opulent public feast 1,000 geese were consumed in a single day.*

not arise until the 18th Dynasty but grew increasingly stronger as Egypt expanded into an empire.

The Egypt of the 18th Dynasty existed in a different world from that of the Old Kingdom, and it therefore required a different organization from that which initially welded together the two lands of Upper and Lower Egypt. The pharaohs of the New Kingdom were constantly planning and frequently going off on military expeditions, so they had to turn more and more of the domestic administration over to subordinates. Furthermore, in the 1,500 years that had elapsed since the unification of the land, the position of the pharaoh and his godship had been modified as the Egyptians had grown in sophistication and the state had become complex. He still summed up total civil, religious and military authority in his person, and the myth of his link with divinity remained, but he came to project as much the image of a man as that of a god. The subordinates eventually developed authority of their own, running as they did sizable civil, temple and military administrations. What began originally as delegated power was gradually transformed into hereditary right.

Of all state, temple and military officials, the most important throughout Egyptian history remained the vizier. He had dozens of titles, among them hereditary prince and count, sealbearer of the king, sole companion to the king; overseer of the fields, the garden, the cows, the serfs, the peasant-farmers and the granaries; steward of the king; overseer of the royal residence; controller of every divine craft and overseer of construction works. He was the chief officer of the state, the only person other than the king who could act in all civil affairs. He presided over the highest court of justice. He saw to the collection of taxes from all over the land and of tribute from abroad. He was the minister of war and the chief of police for the kingdom. He supervised the movement of food and building stones up and down the Nile and oversaw the operation of all public works. The Pharaoh Thutmose III called him "the supporting post of the entire land."

The vizier put in as arduous a day as any modern statesman; he had at least 30 functions to attend to. He was received by the king each morning to get his orders and report on events of the day before. Next he met with his highest-ranking subordinate, the treasurer, who addressed him with a ritual that went: "All thy affairs are sound and prosperous; every responsible incumbent has reported to me, saying: 'All thy affairs are sound and prosperous, the king's house is sound and prosperous.'" The vizier replied to the treasurer in a similar ritual that also began: "All thy affairs are sound and prosperous." Next the vizier went through the ceremony of opening every gate of the palace, "to cause to go in all that goes in, and to go out all that goes out likewise." After this the vizier met with the foremen of construction works, the keepers of the granaries and a series of lesser officials. He examined written reports and dictated replies. Often he traveled at home and abroad in the name of the pharaoh.

For all the scope of his authority, the vizier was not expected to be a tyrant. As spokesman for the pharaoh, he was considered the representative of divine authority, perception and justice, and he was heavily charged with the responsibility to be fair and equitable. His primary role was as chief magistrate, and on his appointment he was customarily exhorted as follows:

"The abomination of the god is a show of partiality. So this is the instruction; thou shalt act accordingly: thou shalt look upon him whom thou knowest like him whom thou dost not know, upon him who is close to thy person like him who is distant from thy house. . . . Do not avoid a petitioner. . . . Thou shalt punish him when thou hast let him hear that on account of which thou punishest him. . . . Be not enraged toward a man unjustly. . . . Behold, if a man show forth the fear of him a myriad of times, there is something of violence in him. . . . Behold, a man shall be in his office [as long as] he shall do things according to that which is given to him." This was a concept of justice and humanity that was remarkable in the ancient world.

When the vizier made his first appearance in Egyptian history, early in the Old Kingdom, he was generally appointed from among the royal princes. Later the office passed to an able member of the nobility, and it often remained within a particular family. But sometimes it went to a qualified man who found favor with the king, and kings did not always restrict such favors to the rich and the well-born. One pharaoh wrote to his son: "Advance thy great men, so that they may carry out thy laws. . . . Great is a great man when his great men are great. . . . Do not distinguish the son of a noble man from a poor man, but take to thyself a man because of the work of his hands."

With such an attitude prevailing among the pharaohs, a few men rose from modest beginnings to positions of authority. A certain Uni, toward the end of the Old Kingdom, began his adult life as keeper of the royal warehouse and advanced from that to become keeper of the grounds for the pharaoh's pyramid, which meant that he was responsible for quarrying and delivering the stones that built the pyramid complex. Later he was made a magistrate, then an army general, then governor of Upper Egypt. He ended his days as royal tutor and companion of the pharaoh.

Uni was able to advance because he was under the eye of the pharaoh; but other men acquired power by exercising initiative far from the capital. The country was divided into more than 40 provinces—or nomes, as the Greeks called them—and each was administered by a governor, or nomarch.

OTHER EXPANDING CULTURES

While Egypt basked in New Kingdom opulence, other societies were also progressing. Most vigorous was the culture of Mycenae, which from 1600 to 1200 B.C. spread from mainland Greece to the shores of Asia Minor. Remnants of that culture —such as the hammered-gold royal death mask shown above, richly painted pottery, and the ruins of massive fortifications and palaces—attest to its wealth, artistry and power. Mycenae, through its numerous colonies in the eastern Mediterranean and through the epic legends of the Trojan War, left a rich heritage for descendants who centuries later shaped classical Greece. The Olympian gods, the concept of *aretē* (the pursuit of excellence) and the Greek language itself found their genesis in the world of Mycenae.

The Mycenaeans were only one of the peoples making history during this age. The Hebrews, having fled Egypt, were conquering the land of Canaan. The Chinese, under the Shang Dynasty, established the basic forms of a graceful calligraphy that has lasted to the present day. And in Asia Minor the Hittites mastered the technique of ironworking—a skill that was eventually to bring the Bronze Age to a close.

Governors charged with the administration of distant areas had to act on their own without permission from the pharaoh, and often without even his knowledge; they developed independence and self-assurance. These were the men who carved out principalities for themselves when the Old Kingdom foundered at the end of the Sixth Dynasty. They ruled their territories as independent princes during the First Intermediate Period and for a time into the Middle Kingdom.

Besides the governors, the Middle Kingdom pharaohs had another limitation on their authority in the persons of the priests. From the end of the Old Kingdom onward the priests grew in wealth and influence, until by the time of the 18th Dynasty they were the richest and strongest men in society and ruled almost in partnership with the pharaoh.

Egyptian legend had an explanation for the power the priests wielded; it was that a prophecy had been uttered to the effect that the royal succession would pass to a son of Re born miraculously to a wife of a priest of that god. In the Fifth Dynasty the pharaoh added the phrase "Son of Re" to his titles, and from that time on, the priests began to exert considerable influence as spokesmen of the god, whose son the pharaoh now was. The first priesthood to become significant was the one that worshiped Re; the next was the priesthood of Ptah of Memphis. Finally, and most powerful of all, came the priests of Amon of Thebes, the god who effected the ousting of the Hyksos and redeemed Egypt for the New Kingdom.

As the priests grew in power the pharaohs found it necessary to assure their support. The pharaohs of the Fifth Dynasty exempted the priests from certain services to the state and from taxes. They were not required to lend their servants to till the fields or to haul the quarried stones for construction work, and they were excused from turning over

WITH SPEARS AND SHIELDS *these wooden soldiers stood guard in the tomb of an Egyptian prince. The model infantrymen reflected the prince's military interests during his life, and they also served as symbols of protection in the afterworld. Each Egyptian soldier had a shield decorated with his own design; when summoned to battle, he could easily identify his own shield.*

to the national coffers a portion of the yield of their lands. These measures added to the priests' wealth and in turn to their power. They also helped to damage the national economy, for they kept from the royal treasury riches that the pharaohs might have used for the state. The time would come when the government would not have sufficient income to keep the people fed.

The exemption from taxes in the Old Kingdom was only the beginning of the priests' acquisition of wealth. By the time of the empire they had become richer still on foreign booty, as the gods were given tribute for every military victory; and hungry for even greater wealth, the priests grew as eager as the pharaohs for further foreign conquest. The pharaohs, for their part, were grateful to the gods for their benevolence, so they continued to add to the estates of the temples. There developed a self-perpetuating cycle in which the priests were the major beneficiaries. By the end of the New Kingdom the high priest of Amon controlled one of the greatest landholdings of the ancient world; some estimates put it as high as 30 per cent of all the land in Egypt.

Wealth and power were not alone responsible for the lofty position of the priesthood. The rise of the gods preceded the expansion of the empire; it was coincident with the ousting of the Hyksos. The presence of the foreign rulers had filled the Egyptians with self-doubts. Now they thanked the gods for their release from the hated alien rule; at the same time, they wanted to stay in the gods' good graces. They willingly gave the gods an active hand in more and more of their affairs.

By the time of the late empire, the gods were making manifest their instructions by "visible signs." "Yes or no" questions must have been put to the effigy in a temple, for texts of that period describe Amon as "nodding" in assent and remaining still or "recoiling" to express disapproval of certain affairs. Since the priests determined the signs of the gods, the new turn of events indicates the mounting authority exercised by the priesthood; it was a great change from the days of the Old Kingdom, when the pharaoh made his decisions alone.

The gods did not confine their activity to imperial conquest, but entered civil affairs as well. In the early days of Egypt when magistrates—who were subordinates of the vizier—tried a civil or criminal offense, they gave their decision as the pharaoh's. By the beginning of the New Kingdom the high priest of Amon sometimes attended court trials, which were held in the temples and presided over by the vizier; and by the time that Ramses III died the gods were intervening, too.

Ramses III was apparently killed as a result of a harem conspiracy. After his death he spoke through an oracle in the temple and directed the court to examine the case and punish the criminals—but he affected for himself and his son, the new Pharaoh, a cool detachment from concern with the outcome. In other words, he had turned over the law— so said the priests—to the magistrates and made them full arbiters in their own right.

The third section of Egyptian society that was vested with power was the professional army. It developed even later than the priesthood, but once it became established, it exercised authority with the blessing of the pharaoh.

Until the time of the New Kingdom, the army was largely a kind of feudal levy that was called upon only in time of need. The pharaoh might keep a small cadre of standing troops, but in an emergency he called upon the provincial nobles to conscript the peasants who normally tended the fields, the canals and the quarries. He put them under the command of a royal son or a member of the nobility, and sent them off to fight for as long as the emergency lasted. When the trouble passed, the levied men would return to their plows and their benches. In the feudal era of the First Intermediate Period, each provincial governor—or prince, as he now was—commanded a similar aggregation periodically recruited from his subjects. Under the rulers of the Middle Kingdom much the same system prevailed.

But driving out the Hyksos at the end of the Second Intermediate Period required organized military effort, and so did building an empire. The men who founded the 18th Dynasty established a professional army. At first this army was commanded by the pharaoh himself, then by the crown prince, and later by career officers. It swelled in time to a military establishment of no mean size: it included a large infantry, transport officers, quartermasters and labor troops. The infantry was trained and disciplined to fight on every kind of terrain and from shipboard if necessary. The army also included a chariotry, for the Egyptians had adopted the horse and chariot from the Hyksos. The chariot troops were the ancient Egyptian equivalent of the cavalry and, like the cavalry in recent times, they formed the most glamorous arm of the service in their day.

For anyone lacking family lineage, the army probably provided the easiest path for advancement in imperial Egypt. As a relatively late arrival, it had neither tradition behind it nor established families who might resist the entry of parvenus. Besides, men have always applauded a victor; an Egyptian who showed valor on the battlefield did not go unhonored. Finally, because the army was new, it had room for new talents; a man who never saw battle might rise through the administration of the army's affairs. And a man who distinguished himself in the army might move into other segments of the society.

One man who did just that was Amenhotep-son-of-Hapu. The father was a man of modest calling,

ANCIENT AIDS TO BEAUTY, *grouped around a mummy's mask and a carved head, reflect the wealthy Egyptian woman's preoccupation with cosmetics and jewelry. The lettered diagram identifies the artifacts, dating from many periods: (a) pots for holding kohl, an eye shadow still used today, (b) sticks for applying kohl, (c) hair tweezers, (d) comb, (e) hair curler, (f) bronze hand mirror, (g) amulet on a string of beads, (h) rings, (i) bead necklaces and collars, (j) wooden cosmetic box, (k) stone and palette for grinding cosmetics. Also shown are a faïence drinking cup at upper left, some alabaster vases at rear (probably used for cosmetics) and a bronze bowl at center.*

but his son became the outstanding official of Amenhotep III, and one of the most prominent figures of the New Kingdom. After serving the army as a scribe he was made responsible for the royal bodyguard, for the collection of taxes, for the defense of the borders, for the transport and erection of two 70-foot statues of Amenhotep III (they still stand in the Theban Necropolis) and for the stewardship of the vast estates of the King's wife and daughter. A queen, as the daughter of a god, the wife of a god and the mother of a god, had always had rank in Egyptian society; by the time of the 18th Dynasty all well-born women had their own rights to property. They could buy and sell, and they could testify in court.

Before Amenhotep-son-of-Hapu died at about the age of 80, he was Overseer of All Works of the King—in other words, the vizier. Amenhotep III so prized his vizier's services that he granted him permission to erect several statues in the temple of Karnak. In all of them he is shown as royal scribe, seated on the ground with an open papyrus on his lap. More striking, the Pharaoh further allowed him to erect a mortuary temple of monumental size next to the royal temples in western Thebes. No man of modest birth had ever been so honored. Amenhotep III endowed the temple of his favorite in perpetuity; mortuary services for him were continued there long after his death, and a cult grew up around this illustrious scribe-turned-army man and vizier. He was revered as one of Egypt's great sages, and proverbs ascribed to him were translated into Greek 12 centuries after his time.

Amenhotep-son-of-Hapu would never have made his mark in the army or anywhere else, of course, if he had not been literate. In his youth, as a scribe, he was one of a large corps of citizens who ranked just below the ruling class. The scribes did yeoman service keeping the machinery of government running—conveying the rulers' commands and recording the many affairs of the state.

Among the most important of these affairs was taxation. Everything in Egypt, like everything in any centralized state, was taxed. The farmer paid on his crops, the herdsman on his herd, the artisan on his handiwork, even the fisherman on his catch and the hunter on his bag. Taxation requires records. There were land surveys classifying all acreage according to productivity, censuses listing every man and his animals, ledgers recording payments and receipts attesting to payments. Since money had not yet been invented, taxes were paid in produce and labor, which made the keeping of records exceedingly complex.

Records require record-keepers, and such men were to be found all over Egypt. There were surveyors in the fields, tax collectors on the threshing floors and in the workshops, receivers of custom duties at the frontiers and census takers at the house doorways.

Most of this vast corps of scribes were employed by the palace, but there were others employed by the army and by the temples. The army needed scribes to log the storing and dispatching of supplies, to enlist recruits, and to send communications into the field and back to the pharaoh. The high priest of Amon and his associates, with vast territories and multitudes of lesser priests to house, feed and supervise, employed thousands of scribes. Amon was not the only deity whose wealth called for voluminous records. Ptah of Memphis and Re of Heliopolis, though they had been superseded by Amon as national god, both had sizable estates, and even the minor deities had temples and temple holdings that required bookkeeping by scribes.

The position of scribe was in theory open to all, but in fact it was probably closed to peasants. It took diligence and doggedness to survive the training, for the curriculum was tedious and the regimen harsh. The masters did not spare the rod, because "a youngster's ear is on his back—he listens when he is beaten," and they exhorted the boys not to frequent beer halls or run after women.

A scribal school was generally attached to a temple, but there was also one at the palace and occasionally secular scribes ran village schools of their own. A student was enrolled at about the age of five. For the next dozen years or so he put in long, tedious hours from sunup to sundown. He wrote and wrote and wrote—most of the time with a brush and ink on a wooden writing board, but sometimes on papyrus, sometimes on a broken bit of limestone or pottery—copying over and over again the same excerpts from classical literature, form letters and endless lists of articles that a government scribe would have to know how to write, such as "wine of Egypt, wine of Palestine, wine of the oases" and "fresh meat, cooked meat, sweetened meat." This was a practice designed "to teach the ignorant to know everything that is."

If he did not learn to know "everything that is," the student did pick up a certain knowledge of geography, history, arithmetic and foreign phrases, and an acquaintance with temple and governmental procedures. It was the products of these scribal schools who managed to rise in a society where rank was for the most part hereditary.

Often the work pieces were propaganda extolling the joys of life as a scribe, which was touted as preferable to any other. Farmers and even priests, these documents said, had to do difficult tasks, but scribes dressed in clean linen, did not have to labor in the fields, and oversaw the work of others. Better still, "their names have become everlasting, even though they themselves are gone. . . . If doors and buildings were constructed, they are crumbled; . . . mortuary service is done . . . tombstones are covered with dirt; and . . . graves are forgotten. But [the] names [of scribes] are still pronounced because of their books which they made . . . and

the memory of them lasts to the limits of eternity. Be a scribe, and put it in your heart that your name may fare similarly."

Although the scribes were not of the ruling class, they worked in close association with it, which meant that their way of life was considerably easier than that of the peasants. Many scribes must have been quartered in the palaces and temple precincts.

Scribes also had unlimited opportunities for graft. A papyrus dated toward the end of the New Kingdom tells of a riverboat captain who looted more than 90 per cent of the grain he contracted to deliver to a certain temple over a period of nine years. It is not recorded whether the man was eventually brought before the law or not. In any event, he clearly could not have engaged in thievery on so grand a scale without buying the silence of many—not only the scribes who registered the grain at the temple, but also of all the others involved in the transaction from the moment the grain left the farmers' fields.

The nobility, the priesthood, the army and the bureaucracy, as large as they may have been, together constituted the lesser portion of Egypt's total population. In the time of the pharaohs—as in Egypt today—the vast majority were the masses who toiled in the workshops and plowed the fields. Of these, the skilled and semiskilled workers stood on a plane higher in the social order than their unskilled brethren and the peasants on the farms.

The pharaoh, the nobles and the priests kept draftsmen, quarriers, masons, carpenters, bricklayers, sculptors and painters busy on their palaces, temples and tombs. The court had work for goldsmiths, jewelers, weavers and cabinetmakers. The army needed the services of chariot makers, armorers, leather workers and boatbuilders. These men were by and large fine craftsmen and many were true artists.

Their talents brought them a better standard of living than the peasants who tilled the fields. Near the Valley of the Kings, for example, at the site of Deir el Medineh, stood a village that for almost 500 years housed the workers who built and decorated the tombs of the pharaohs. Excavations at the site have turned up thousands of bills, accounts, receipts and letters scratched on chips of limestone and pottery and on scraps of papyrus. From these fragments and other evidence at Deir el Medineh emerges a picture of the life of Egyptian artisans during the age of the empire.

Their dwellings were constructed of unbaked brick. Working conditions were by no means brutally harsh, and the work shifts were divided into 10-day periods. There seems to have been considerable leniency about time off; it was allowed not only for sickness but also for tending the sick. Sickness itself was liberally interpreted; there is at least one case on record of a man's being excused from work because he had been beaten up by his wife.

Wages were paid in produce—bread, beer, beans, onions, dried meat, fat and salt. The various crafts were graded and their wages determined accordingly. Foremen and scribes were the highest paid; then draftsmen, sculptors, painters; then quarriers and masons; and finally unskilled laborers, those who dug and lifted and hauled.

Akhenaton took exemplary care of his craftsmen at the new city he built at Akhetaton. He provided villas with studios attached for his court sculptors, and he placed their assistants in more modest but pleasant dwellings nearby.

In stable times there were not a few men in the skilled crafts such as drafting and sculpturing who earned enough to build themselves well-appointed tombs. In bad times, on the other hand, the artisan was probably worse off than the peasant, for corrupt government officials might withhold the arti-

san's pay, and when they did the artisan went hungry. This was particularly true in the latter part of the New Kingdom, when the fortunes of Egypt began to wane and the national treasury was low.

In about 1170 B.C. the government fell two months behind in the payment of wages. Suddenly one day the workers at the Necropolis in Thebes threw down their tools and walked off the job, chanting: "We are hungry! We are hungry!" They marched to the Ramesseum, the mortuary temple of Ramses II, and sat down outside the walls, on the edge of the cultivated fields. They refused to move, even when three officials implored them to go back to work. The next day they marched out again, and on the third they invaded the enclosure around the temple proper. They were orderly but determined. That day their rations for one month were delivered, but they continued the strike for eight days, until the full payment for both months was delivered. This was the first recorded strike in history, and it is an indication that the lower classes of Egypt may not have been so passive as they have sometimes been depicted.

There were other strikes in the months that followed, but when the people did not get their rations they turned more and more to robbing the tombs by night and selling the loot for grain. Tomb robbing had always beset the pharaohs, but by the reign of Ramses IX, when the people were desperate, it had become a way of life. It was done with the connivance of many government officials, who fattened their own incomes by accepting bribes. Tomb robbers were periodically arrested, but they often bought their way out of jail and returned to robbing.

Although the artisans were a level above the peasants in the social pyramid, the peasants may nevertheless have had the better luck in bad times. When the artisan had no pay he went hungry; but even in the worst of times the peasant was generally able to wrest enough from the soil to eat.

Today's fellahin, the peasants of modern Egypt, lead much the same life their forebears led millennia ago. The peasants of ancient Egypt were not slaves; they were free tenant farmers who worked the land for the pharaoh, a noble or a temple of priests. The lion's share of the grain, wheat and flax that the peasants produced went to their landlords, and they kept for themselves only a small portion as wages. What they did not eat they might barter for some small luxury such as a little statue or an amulet.

Their life was for the most part an unchanging round of spreading freshly deposited Nile mud, plowing, planting, hauling water for irrigation and harvesting, threshing, delivering to the granaries and, in the time of the drought, mending dikes and clearing clogged canals. During floodtime they might be called from the fields to serve on the work parties of the pharaoh's construction projects. They were dependent, like the animals they husbanded, on the landlords. Their lot was the routine of the peasant's life—and its rewards, which no doubt were greater under Egypt's clear skies and agreeable clime than in some of the ancient world's less favored lands.

There is little documentation concerning the life of the peasants; the picture of their disposition and their life must be surmised from the drawings and inscriptions in the tombs, and these were put there by their masters, not by the peasants. From the volume of tedious work they are shown doing, it would appear that the peasants must have been diligent, and from the songs that survive, that they must have been good-natured as well. Driving cattle through the swamp, they sang to the crocodiles and the fish, and threshing or reaping they sang in antiphonal chorus, rejoicing in the beauty of the sky and the breath of the north wind.

And there was periodic variation in their general routine. Floodtime was also the season of the great religious festivals, when the images of the gods were carried through the land in pomp and pageantry. During the celebrations, the peasants had a holiday, and they probably dined at feasts given by the landowners whose fields they tilled.

Below the peasants, at the base of the Egyptian social pyramid, were the slaves. There had always been slaves in Egypt's history, but their numbers greatly increased in the age of the New Kingdom, when foreign conquests brought in prisoners of war.

The least fortunate slaves of all were conscripted to work in the dreadful gold and copper mines of Nubia, the Sudan and Sinai, where, according to the Greeks, water was rationed and men dropped by scores in the torrid heat. But some were absorbed into the army, and others were assigned to labor on the estates of the nobles and the priests. According to one document, Ramses III is said to have given 113,000 slaves to the temples during the course of his reign. The more fortunate ones found their way into menial service for the royal family or the nobility, where they generally fared better than the native Egyptian peasantry. The children of a few of these, with exceptional ability, made themselves indispensable to their masters and rose to good positions in the bureaucracy—and there, if they had aspirations, they might hope to begin the ascent that others of the bureaucracy had made before them.

Probably few Egyptians thought of ascent per se, for they envisioned their society—as they did their universe, their gods and their afterlife—as an endless continuum in which change was not to be expected. Still, if their social order was generally fixed and hereditary, it was nevertheless subject to occasional flux. It shifted with the winds—ever changing and ever changeless.

A BEREAVED FAMILY, *in an ancient tomb painting, clusters around the bearded figure of a departed official as his son (right) offers him votive gifts.*

A LEISURED ELITE

The highest earthly goal of the Egyptian aristocrat was to grow in the pharaoh's esteem and reap the rewards of royal favor. The upper class formed a small, closed society: a hereditary caste of priests, soldiers and bureaucrats who collected taxes, supervised public works, dispensed justice and performed the voluminous paperwork of the highly centralized government. A rare commoner might curry favor with the pharaoh and rise into this charmed circle—one man of modest beginnings rose to be Royal Architect; another, the keeper of a government storehouse, became Governor of half of Egypt. But literacy, nepotism and marriages among nobles were all barriers to social mobility. Within the upper class, a noble's office and estate were held by grace of the pharaoh. Even great lords treated the pharaoh as a god. The rulers, however, sometimes took a more worldly view of their position. One Pharaoh, Achthoes II, dryly commented: "royalty is a good profession."

THE OPULENCE AND ORDER OF A GREAT HOUSE

A noble's estate, like this one at Tell el Amarna, was far more than a family dwelling. It was built around workshops, stables, shrines and banquet rooms. Servants were constantly busy—baking bread in the kitchens, bottling beer in the household brewery, storing grain in silos. There were scribes, vintners, carpenters and herdsmen. The whole establishment was managed with the Egyptian passion for order. Although the household was run by the noble's steward, there is evidence that his wife also had a free hand—"You should not supervise . . . your wife in her house," one father admonished his son.

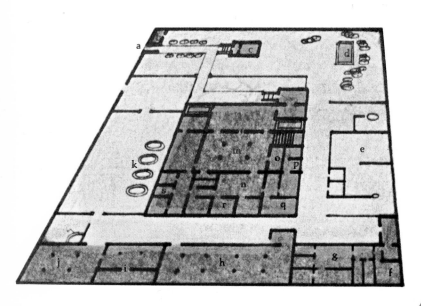

a. MAIN ENTRANCE	k. GRAIN SILOS
b. CARETAKER'S LODGE	l. ENTRANCE HALL AND LOGGIA
c. CHAPEL	m. MAIN HALL
d. POOL AND GARDEN	n. HAREM
e. COWPENS	o. STOREROOM
f. KITCHEN	p. LAVATORIES
g. STOREROOM	q. MAIN BEDROOM
h. SERVANTS' QUARTERS	r. GUEST ROOMS
i. TACK ROOM AND WORKSHOP	s. BEDROOMS
j. STABLES	t. WEST LOGGIA

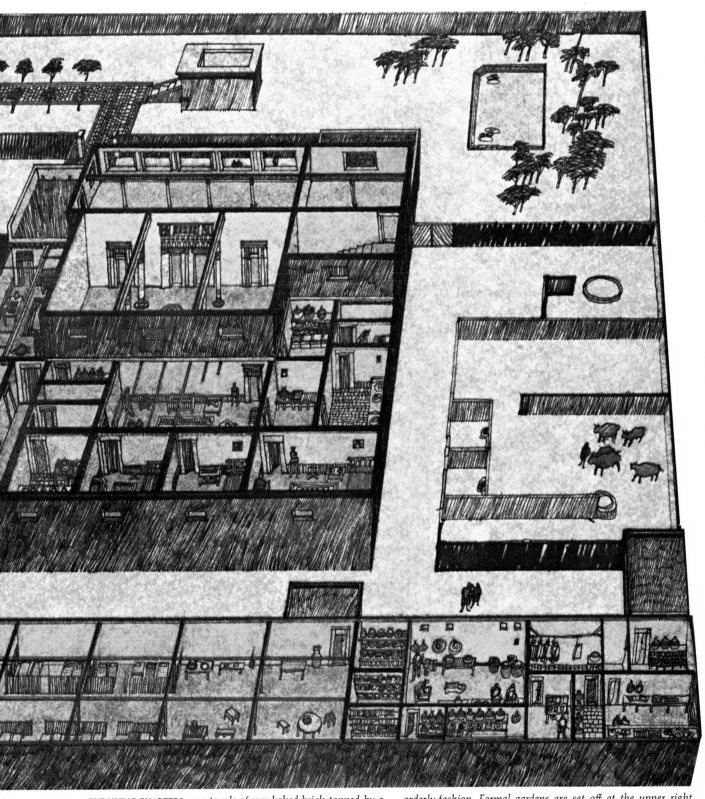

THE LIVING QUARTERS, *a rectangle of sun-baked brick topped by a loggia, stood at the center of an Egyptian estate. This schematic drawing shows how the grounds were divided in an efficient,* orderly fashion. Formal gardens are set off at the upper right, cowpens at the rear of the house. Workrooms, kitchens, servants' quarters and stables are crowded together in the foreground.

PLAYING A HARP, *a servant adds a pleasant note to the daily life of a noble house. For banquets a professional harpist was hired.*

THE SERVANTS' ROLE

Servants were essential to the well-run, noble Egyptian household. Some, trained in personal service, worked as maids, played musical instruments about the house, or tended to banquet guests. Others were employed outside the main house, cooking, baking, washing the laundry or working in the fields. Servants were frequently foreigners, Nubians and Asiatics taken in war. Others may have been bought in slave markets. Although servants destined for a lord's household or his harem were highly prized and often very costly, they did not always live in harmony—some Egyptian paintings depict servant girls fighting among themselves.

ADJUSTING AN EARRING, *a slave girl aids a guest at a banquet. A host of servants labored at helping noblewomen look their best.*

A FERTILE SOURCE OF WEALTH

Egypt's noble way of life depended on agriculture, both for commodities and tax revenues. The entire process depicted in this painting was directed by a host of officials who supervised the irrigation system and the harvest, and who saw that a proper share of the crop went to temple and government granaries. The painting employs a traditional ancient device of registers, or rows, to show various steps in harvesting wheat (the rows are read in sequence from bottom left to top right).

In the first row, workers reap wheat with sickles and carry it in rope baskets to a threshing building. There the sheaves are raked out into a thick carpet of wheat.

In the middle register, right to left, oxen tread kernels out of the husks. Next, peasants winnow the wheat, tossing it up in scoops so that the wind will blow away the chaff. In a kiosk to the left stands Menna, a scribe of the fields of the late 14th Century B.C., in whose tomb the painting was discovered. At the far end of the register, four subordinate scribes record the yield on their tablets.

In the top register, from left to right, an official unwinds a measuring rope as he surveys the land; such surveys were made to estimate how much grain per acre was owed in taxes. In the center of the register Menna appears again. Here he watches one of his agents beat a farmer late in paying his taxes. Others stand in line, probably waiting to be punished.

The entire painting is illuminated with realistic, human details. In the middle register the winnowers have covered their heads against the sun and dust. In the bottom row a laborer rests under a tree while another plays the flute. To the left of them two little girls engage in a fierce bout of hair-pulling, fighting over bits of wheat that the reapers have left behind.

FASHIONABLE LADIES *offer whiffs of fragrant lotus blossoms to one another, as a slave girl passes around a dish of refreshments. Ladies were usually, though not always, seated apart from the men, on the opposite side of the large banquet room.*

VINEYARD WORKERS *pluck and tread grapes on a noble's estate, preparing the fine wines that a lord served at his banquets. Egyptian wines were labeled with date, vineyard and variety—for the convenience of tax assessors, not connoisseurs.*

SCENTS AND WINES

Feasts were a frequent and often disorderly diversion of the wealthy Egyptian. Guests drank quantities of beer and wine, and feasted on pigeon, duck, oxen, and some of Egypt's 40 varieties of breads and cakes. Women sat with cones of greasy perfumed incense on their elegant coiffures *(above)*; as the party wore on, the slowly melting grease bathed head and shoulders in a sticky, sweet-smelling pomade. For all the display of elegance, banquets often grew raucous. Schoolboys were admonished against dissipating themselves at these banquets: "Look at you," a teacher cried, "beside a pretty girl, drenched in perfume . . . beating your stomach, reeling and rolling about on the ground."

THE MANY MOODS OF AN EGYPTIAN BANQUET

The formal banquets of Egypt were many-sided affairs, ranging from gay entertainments to occasional morbid ceremonies. Hired dwarfs, wrestlers or storytellers might enliven the first course. Dancing girls, often selected from the noble's own harem, would follow, alternating between slow, erotic dances and wild acrobatic stunts—the complex Egyptian choreography included splits, pirouettes, cart-wheels, somersaults and backbends. The guests at these affairs often ate and drank themselves sick—one tomb painting portrays a prostrate guest being carried out by his friends. At some banquets, though, the host finally threw a damper on the festivities. According to Herodotus, some hosts brought out a carved wooden mummy set in a small coffin—to remind everyone of his eventual destiny.

CROUCHING SINGERS *chant hymns to the reedy accompaniment of woodwinds. The two singers shown at center are holding up their hands to give the instrumentalists their cue.*

DANCING IN UNISON, *a line of girls is spurred on by two clapping musicians. The weighted disk swinging from the end of each dancer's pigtail accentuates the rhythm of the dance.*

SPORT FOR THE FAMILY

Fowling and fishing amidst the tall papyrus reeds along the banks of the Nile was a sport enjoyed by the whole family, as shown in this ancient portrayal, a stock scene in Egyptian tomb paintings. At left, the noble hurls throwing sticks at a

flock of geese; at right, his upraised hand may have held a spear, now hurled. In this scene the lord's wife clings to his waist, a daughter to his leg (a stylized way of depicting the family group). Another daughter appears in the background, imitating her father's hunting form. The family often took a civet along on these outings to flush birds out of the reeds. For rougher sport, a noble rode into the desert to hunt gazelle and antelope, taking along a pack of trained hunting dogs.

6

A MAJESTIC ART

The art of a people is their statement of what they believe, hope and cherish. It also tells a history, for it reflects the shifting fortunes and the changing concerns of a nation.

The architects, sculptors and painters who created the art of ancient Egypt bear comparison with those of any age. Their achievements not only reached esthetic heights, but they represent technological marvels as well, for the Egyptians executed their masterpieces with the most rudimentary of tools. The remarkable record of their artistic excellence can be read in works as majestic as their great temples and as delicate as their intricate jeweled clasps.

Little is known about the homes of the Egyptians because they constructed them chiefly out of bricks made from mud and set them on low ground. In time these dwellings became overlaid with silt from the flooding river; consequently none have survived. But more important to the Egyptians than their homes, which were merely for temporary residence, were their graves, in which they expected to spend eternity. The graves the Egyptians built, together with the decoration and furnishings they gave them, provide a better record of their beliefs, hopes and ideals—and, consequently, of their art—than that of any other civilization of the ancient world. In particular, the burial places of the Egyptian pharaohs offered the nation's architects a challenge as well as an opportunity, and they accepted both eagerly.

Prehistoric graves were covered with mounds of sand or heaps of loose stones, as much to preserve the bodies from exposure as to mark the sites. But the persistent desert wind blew away the sand, and jackals foraged among the stones, so safer grave coverings had to be devised by all early peoples. At the beginning of the dynastic era the Egyptians learned to build mastabas—flat-topped, slope-sided tombs made of mud brick. The word "mastaba" is modern Arabic for "bench"; the tombs are so called because they resemble the benches that stand outside Egyptian houses.

The Egyptians decorated their mastabas by arranging the outside bricks in geometric patterns. Within, and usually below ground, were several chambers—one for the body and others for the articles

MASSIVE COLUMNS, *33 feet around and 69 feet high, exemplify the awesome proportions of Amon's temple at Karnak. This part was built by two New Kingdom pharaohs. The decorations show kings making offerings to gods.*

that were left for the dead. In time the mastabas grew larger—some may have been as tall as 17 feet —and more intricately arranged. A pharaoh of the First Dynasty had the floor of his burial pit laid with limestone, which was quarried from the nearby desert hills, and one of the Second Dynasty lined the whole burial chamber with it. In the course of time, some mastabas were built with as many as 30 chambers.

Soon the Egyptians were making more extensive use of limestone. In the Third Dynasty they built the world's first structure made entirely of stone, the Step Pyramid at Sakkarah. It was constructed for the Pharaoh Djoser by Imhotep, an architect who became as famous as the Pharaoh he meant to immortalize; Imhotep is also credited in legend with having been a writer and a physician. Centuries after he lived, the Greeks identified him with Asclepius, their god of medicine.

The Step Pyramid that Imhotep created was really a series of six mastabas set one on top of another, and the stones he used were small blocks laid together like bricks. But it was a mammoth monument that dwarfed all other mastabas; it measured 413 by 344 feet at the base and stood about 200 feet high. It had underground chambers, plus courts and chapels outside it, that were carefully decorated with limestone columns embellished with carved plant designs, carved ceilings simulating wooden roofing logs, and carved walls made to resemble the reed matting that covered the walls of Egyptian houses.

One new idea breeds another, and less than two centuries later Imhotep's successors had reared the first true pyramids, massive structures of large stone blocks arranged to rise evenly to a point. The most celebrated are the pyramids that stand today at Gizeh immortalizing Khufu, Khafre and Menkaure (or Cheops, Chephren and Mycerinus) of the Fourth Dynasty.

For the Egyptians to have conceived the structures at all was imaginative; to have executed them was heroic, for they had to cut rock with the simplest of copper and stone tools and to move massive blocks into place with muscle, since they did not have block and tackle. It took inspiration to conceive the pyramids, and superb skill and organization to achieve them.

The first of the structures at Gizeh, the one belonging to Khufu and the largest of the three, now stands about 450 feet high, but it was originally probably 30 feet higher when its capstone and outer facing were in place; both of these were later stripped away by the Egyptians themselves for use in other construction.

The great age of pyramid building lasted about 400 years, from the time of the Fourth Dynasty through the Sixth. Pyramids continued to be built after that, though on a smaller scale, and to be used by the pharaohs as tombs for about another 400 years. At the end of the Middle Kingdom they were largely abandoned by the pharaohs.

In the Middle Kingdom, when the emphasis began to shift from glorifying the god-king alone to glorifying him in company with the other gods, the burial markers for the kings began to undergo a change in design. Nebhepetre Mentuhotep, the most prominent Pharaoh of the 11th Dynasty (he reunified the land after the First Intermediate Period) raised for himself at Deir el Bahri, near Thebes, a thoroughly original funerary monument that was an ambitious complex built against a rock cliff, arranged in three levels and landscaped with trees. At the entrance to the complex was a great court with a portico. From this court a ramp led up to a porticoed terrace, and that in turn led up to another terrace. At the top a pyramid rose over the whole structure, but this pyramid was not the tomb; the tomb proper lay at the rear of the complex, where it was carved into the living rock. Standing and seated

MAKING MUD BRICKS, *artisans of the New Kingdom use a process still employed along the Nile. In a frieze from Thebes one workman is up to his knees in a mixture of mud and chaff. Others shape the clayey mass with a wooden form; the soft bricks are dried under the burning sun until rock-hard. Ancient Egypt's most common building material, brick was used to house the living; stone was reserved for the tombs of the dead and temples of the gods. The Egyptian word for brick, "tobe," is the origin of the modern word "adobe."*

statues lined the way across the courtyard leading to the temple. Only one structure besides Mentuhotep's survives from the Middle Kingdom—a small chapel built by Amenemhet III at Medinet Madi—largely because the vigorous pharaohs of the New Kingdom altered or rebuilt whatever else remained when they came to power.

In the New Kingdom two kinds of temple proliferated: the mortuary temple, devoted to the cult of the dead pharaoh, and the temple to a god, in which the cult image of the god was housed and in which his worship and services took place. Some of the latter were major temples in themselves; others, dedicated to Amon, were way stations for the god on his periodic journeys from his major temple at Karnak to another temple during one of the many festivals.

Among the most famous and loveliest of mortuary temples is the one Hatshepsut had built for herself at Deir el Bahri, next to the temple of Mentuhotep, which served as her inspiration. Unlike some of the early pyramids, which were designed piecemeal and for which the plans were altered many times in the building, Hatshepsut's temple was planned and completed as a unit. It remains today much as it must have looked in her time, because later rulers made fewer alterations than they did in other temples. The architect (who was Senmut, Hatshepsut's court favorite) achieved a triumph of setting and design; the edifice seems to flow directly out of the majestic cliffs that stand behind it. He skillfully varied the shape and arrangement of columns and carefully integrated with them more than 190 statues and relief carvings glorifying the Queen's divine birth and describing the expedition to Punt. This remarkable undertaking, which seems to have carried Egyptian traders to the neighborhood of present-day Somalia, was among the major enterprises of her reign. The reliefs in many tombs and temples are so placed that they have to be seen

IN PRAISE OF A TEMPLE

The pharaohs who built Egypt's temples sought to honor the gods not only with massive construction but also with works of art. On the temples they commissioned, the kings often erected huge stone tablets inscribed with hieroglyphs. These steles were meant primarily to advertise the monarch's zeal in serving the gods, but they also conveyed his proud appreciation of the artistic qualities of the shrines. The stele inscription below boasts of the adornment of a temple at Thebes built by Amenhotep III.

*Behold, the heart of his majesty was
satisfied with making a very great
monument; never has happened the like
since the beginning. He made it as his
monument for his father, Amon, lord of
Thebes, making for him an august temple
on the west of Thebes, an eternal,
everlasting fortress of fine white sandstone,
wrought with gold throughout; its
floor is adorned with silver, all its portals
with electrum [an alloy of gold and
silver]; it is made very wide and large,
and established forever; and adorned with
this very great monument [i.e., the
stele on which the inscription appears].
It contains numerous royal statues,
of Elephantine granite, of costly gritstone,
of every splendid costly stone, established
as everlasting works. Their stature
shines more than the heavens, their rays
are in the faces of men like the sun, when he
shines early in the morning. It is
supplied with a "Station of the King,"
wrought with gold and many costly stones.
Flagstaffs are set up before it, wrought
with electrum; it resembles the horizon in
heaven when Re rises therein. Its lake is filled
with the great Nile, lord of fish and fowl.*

in semidarkness, but Hatshepsut's can be seen in the light, thanks to Senmut's ingenious arrangement.

The temples of the gods were massive walled structures laid out on one level and almost always made of sandstone. Esthetically, they were designed to be enjoyed from the inside on ceremonial occasions rather than from the outside as decoration of the landscape. Their basic features were a pylon (two truncated pyramids forming a monumental gateway); a roofless colonnaded court; a lofty covered hall with a ceiling borne on mighty sandstone columns; and the private sanctuary of the god, which was concealed behind walls and surrounded by small service chambers. The bastionlike pylon discouraged intruders, and the public, when it was allowed in, was not permitted beyond the courtyard. These basic features were repeated in building after building, but with such variations that no two buildings were exactly alike in size, proportion or ground plan.

The temple itself was vast, but it formed only a part of an even greater complex. The complex included living quarters, workshops, a school, a sacred pool, granaries and other storehouses—in short, all the facilities required to support the large and varied community that served the god.

The largest and best-known of these temples is the Temple of Amon at Karnak, on the east bank of the Nile just north of Thebes. It grew out of a modest shrine that was erected in the 12th Dynasty for Amon when he was only an obscure local deity. From the 18th Dynasty on, as the empire expanded and national gratitude toward Amon deepened, almost every pharaoh added to the temple in commemoration of foreign victories. Eventually, the temple complex covered an area that measured about 400 by 500 yards. The architecture—save for the use of imperishable stone instead of short-lived mud brick—was the same as that of the pharaohs' palaces, for this was Amon's palace.

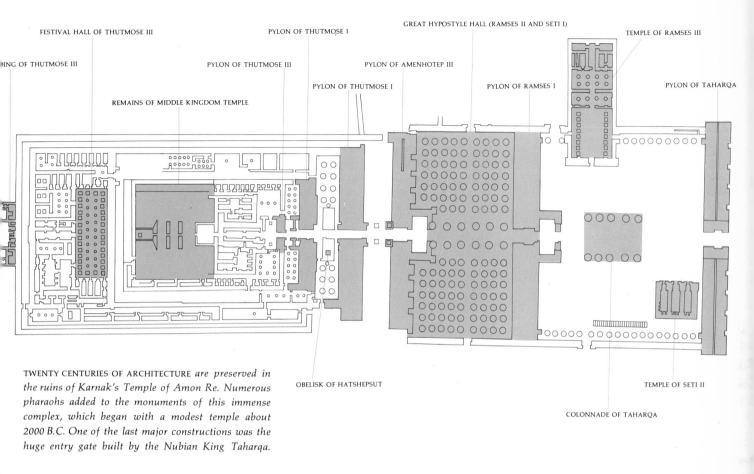

FESTIVAL HALL OF THUTMOSE III

DING OF THUTMOSE III

PYLON OF THUTMOSE I

PYLON OF THUTMOSE III

REMAINS OF MIDDLE KINGDOM TEMPLE

PYLON OF THUTMOSE I

GREAT HYPOSTYLE HALL (RAMSES II AND SETI I)

PYLON OF AMENHOTEP III

PYLON OF RAMSES I

TEMPLE OF RAMSES III

PYLON OF TAHARQA

OBELISK OF HATSHEPSUT

TEMPLE OF SETI II

COLONNADE OF TAHARQA

TWENTY CENTURIES OF ARCHITECTURE *are preserved in the ruins of Karnak's Temple of Amon Re. Numerous pharaohs added to the monuments of this immense complex, which began with a modest temple about 2000 B.C. One of the last major constructions was the huge entry gate built by the Nubian King Taharqa.*

The basic features of the Karnak temple were laid out by Thutmose I, Hatshepsut and Thutmose III, but the most imposing structures still standing at Karnak today are the work of pharaohs who came after the 18th Dynasty. To the complex that was already there, Seti I and his son Ramses II of the 19th Dynasty added another lofty hall—the great Hypostyle Hall (from the Greek, meaning "resting on pillars"). There were 134 pillars standing like giant tree trunks in a forest, all of them carved with scenes depicting the King worshiping Amon. The hall is impressive for its size, but it lacks the grace and light of Hatshepsut's temple. Other rulers, right down to the time of the Greeks, continued to add pylons, courts, shrines and statues to the temple complex.

About two miles south of Karnak, near the modern town of Luxor, stands a second great temple to Amon. Despite the fact that a later pharaoh added an outer court and pylon which are not properly

aligned with the original part of the structure, the temple of Luxor is for the most part more harmonious and coherent in design than that of Karnak. One reason for this is that it reflects the taste of one man, Amenhotep III of the 18th Dynasty, under whom Egyptian craftsmanship and taste reached a very high level. Its graceful columns produce shadowed patterns that are as beautiful as the columns themselves.

A great many of the ancient structures standing in Egypt today were built at the direction of Ramses II, who had an insatiable appetite for building. While professing homage to his predecessors, he usurped without compunction the stone in their buildings, expropriated their memorials and had his own name carved on them. (Other pharaohs had done the same, but not so extensively as he.) By Ramses' time the artistic grace and proportion of Egyptian architecture were giving way to massiveness—perhaps indicating the swelling pride the

Egyptians felt as they enlarged their empire and their sway over the ancient world. Thus, in the first court of the Ramesseum, his mortuary temple at Thebes, Ramses placed a statue of himself that was more than 57 feet tall. It was hewn from heavy red granite and weighed about a thousand tons. The head of this colossus measures more than six feet from ear to ear. Of even greater size are the four giant statues that dominate the façade of one of Ramses II's two temples at Abu Simbel: each of them stands 65 feet high.

The gods' temples were ancient Egypt's last great architectural contribution. After the time of Ramses II, building continued, but architecturally it was a variation on the same theme. Ramses III repeated the design of the Ramesseum for his mortuary temple at Medinet Habu, and similar structures continued to be built by the conquerors during Egypt's days of bondage. The temple of Horus at Edfu—which is in almost perfect condition today—was erected by Greek rulers between the Third and First Centuries B.C. The temple to Isis on the isle of Philae, which is now submerged under the lake at Aswan, was built by Ptolemaic kings and Roman emperors. All of these were modeled on the temple devised by the 18th Dynasty.

As for the decorations of the tombs and temples —statuary, carved relief and painting—one of their most notable characteristics was their resistance to change. Three factors contributed to this. First, the aim of Egyptian art was primarily religious, and religion by its nature clings to tradition. Second, the pharaoh was from the outset the chief patron and the most exalted subject of art. Adornment for temples and tombs was made on his order; the artists worked as artisans, not as free agents, and they were expected to meet specifications, not to innovate. Third, the Egyptians were temperamentally conservative. All these elements worked together to produce an artistic vision that

forever sought to remain changeless, not to depart from tradition. As a result, there is a superficial sameness about Egyptian art—a quality that makes it distinctly Egyptian, despite variations in detail that mark the periods of Old, Middle and New Kingdoms.

Egyptian sculpture arose from the most primitive beginnings, the fashioning of statues that were intended by the early Egyptians to embody for eternity the people they portrayed. Most of the statues found in early tombs were placed facing an opening in the wall, presumably so the spirit could watch the offerings made in his chapel and participate in the services. Because the sole object was the incorporation of the dead man's spirit, sculpture was from the outset the foremost medium for artistic embellishment.

The Old Kingdom developed most of the canons that Egyptian sculpture was to observe throughout its long history. In that age, after some experimentation, the basic poses were established. Egyptian artists did not concern themselves with trying to capture fleeting emotions. The sculptor who was commissioned to make a statue for the god-king's tomb and embody his spirit for eternity attempted to show the essence of the subject and not the wrinkles on his face. Egyptian figures, consequently, are motionless and devoid of passion. If the statues expressed no emotion, however, they did convey character and majesty, and Egyptian sculpture can offer, as a consequence, some of the most impressive portraiture that has ever been wrought in stone.

The figure is generally shown seated, with its hands on its knees, or standing with one foot forward and the hands held straight at the sides or folded across the breast—a stately pose intended to suggest the majesty of the pharaoh. If the statue is of the pharaoh together with his wife, the wife extends her arm around his waist—an indication of

SOLID AND DURABLE, *this 18th Dynasty block statue of an official named Satepihu reflects the massive architectural and sculptural traditions of the Middle and New Kingdoms. The head is clearly defined, the torso and limbs only suggested. Block statues were popular because the large flat surfaces could be filled with hieroglyphs praising the subject.*

the position a queen held as partner to her husband. If the statue is of a scribe, he sits crossed-legged holding a papyrus in his lap. Some figures are shown kneeling in sacrifice while holding offerings in both hands. With minor variations, these poses would be repeated throughout Egypt's artistic history.

If the poses remained fixed, the details of treatment did not, and it is in these that the shifts in political fortunes and the social order are reflected. In the untroubled era of the Old Kingdom, when the pharaoh ruled alone as god and all the world seemed to move at his command, the body of a young ruler had the sleek, muscular physique of an athlete. Elderly nobles were shown as being corpulent and self-satisfied. The face of a pharaoh was detached, serene, confident and majestic. By the beginning of the Middle Kingdom, when priests and provincial governors were limiting the power of the pharaoh and he was coming to seem as much a man as a god, the artists no longer strove for majestic detachment in the portrait of the pharaoh, but tried to personalize it. Consequently, the faces of the early Middle Kingdom pharaohs, those who achieved peace in the land after the era of chaos, seem to show in their statuary the arrogance of conquerors. The faces of the later Middle Kingdom rulers are characterized by weariness and sternness, as if weighed down by the responsibility of rule. Thus, these statues show not only the Egyptians' mastery of the techniques of carving stone, but also an intuition into human character.

The New Kingdom brought another change in the sculpture. The yoke of the Hyksos had been thrown off at the end of the Second Intermediate Period, and the Egyptians were in an expansive mood as they conquered the world and flourished economically. Growing wealth and luxury led to a softening of severity in art, to sophistication, and finally to a self-conscious seeking after effect. In the time of Amenhotep III, when armed conquest had been supplanted by diplomacy and the country was governed from a sumptuous court, the sculpture was given a delicacy and refinement quite different in spirit from the simple, straightforward spareness of the Old Kingdom; by the time of Ramses II this refinement had given way to massiveness in statuary as it had in architecture.

Besides statuary there was a second medium of tomb and temple decoration, carved relief, which was meant to re-create life for the dead man. In general the relief, like the statuary, was done in formal and conventional forms. A pharaoh is rendered as a giant among pygmies; he is shown with his head and legs in profile, but with his chest, shoulders and one eye turned toward the viewer. A herd of cattle is shown in a formal line so there could be no mistaking its number or condition, rather than as a confused mass of heads and bodies and legs as it would appear in life. Such conventions, and not the wish to recapture nature, are the language of Egyptian artists. Perspective, foreshortening, complicated overlapping and all the devices that other artists have used to show spatial relationships are almost totally lacking in Egyptian relief. Such devices are intended to achieve the illusion of reality, whereas Egyptian art was designed to convey a message. A pharaoh had to appear as a god and an all-powerful lord; it was unthinkable to render him in perspective because then he might appear small in scale, and viewers might not know he was the pharaoh. Naturalism appeared only late in Egyptian art, and then chiefly in small details, for naturalism obscures instead of making definite statements.

Toward the end of the Old Kingdom, Egyptian relief underwent some experiment and change. The pictures became more animated. Secondary subjects, such as servants, laborers and animals were most affected; the treatment of principals, and es-

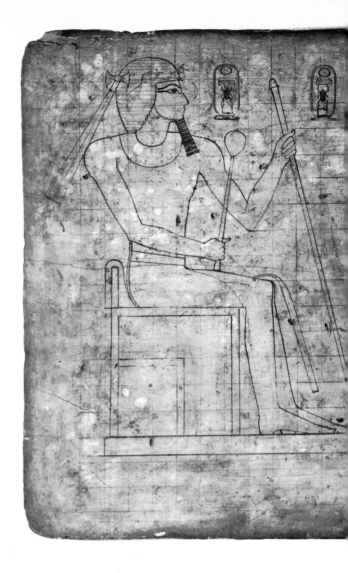

pecially the pharaoh, tended to be prescribed by tradition. Nevertheless, this was an era when the pharaohs were weakening, and perhaps the artists, like the provincial governors, felt the stirrings of self-assertiveness and dared to allow themselves more freedom; in any event, they had less direction from the ruler than before. To some extent their experimentation is noticeable in the statues, but it is more apparent in the reliefs carved on the walls of tombs. In these reliefs the figures are done with rough vigor, and the suggestion of movement begins to appear.

The expansion of the upper class in the Middle Kingdom and the diminishing of the concept of the pharaoh's divinity, which opened the doors of the afterlife to an ever larger segment of society, greatly increased the demand for art and expanded the field of patrons. As a result, the level of craftsmanship varied.

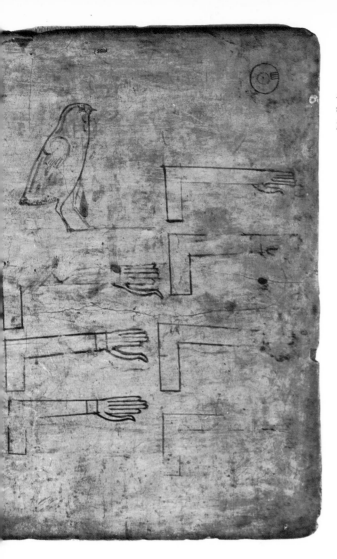

A PRELIMINARY SKETCH *for a painting reveals the deliberation that went into Egyptian art works. The grid ensured that the king's figure would have the exact proportions prescribed by tradition.*

plantlike designs. From the Third Dynasty there was painted a picture of a crocodile lying in wait for a group of animals crossing a swamp—the earliest surviving example of the scenes from life that became so common in later relief and painting. Before the Fourth Dynasty the Egyptians were combining paint and wall carvings. Painting on plaster was cheaper and quicker than carving, and they sometimes rushed a tomb to completion, if the owner died unexpectedly, by omitting the relief. In the New Kingdom, although it continued to be used in conjunction with sculpture, painting became an independent art medium. By that time the Egyptians had the use of almost every color of the spectrum. They were also beginning to paint with curved lines, by means of which they were able—as they were in their reliefs—to suggest movement.

From the outset, the Egyptian painter was as dexterous with the brush as the sculptor was with the chisel. As early as the Fourth Dynasty he could render feathers and fur with stippling and with shadings of color. He indicated no spatial relationships and summarized backgrounds with a few trees or the upright stems of a papyrus plant. But the Egyptian painter is unrivaled in the ancient world, and he left the most complete record of the development of early painting.

The paint that ancient Egyptians used was much the same as what is called tempera today, a mixture of pigment and water with wax or glue as a binder. The pigments were minerals, which is why many of the colors remain remarkably fresh. Carbon was used for black; ochers (iron ore) for brown, red and yellow; powdered malachite (copper ore) for green; and chalk or gypsum for white.

When a mural was to be painted, the rock on which it was to be executed was covered with plaster, and the paint was applied after the plaster had set. Then a preserving coat of wax or clear varnish was added.

In the late New Kingdom not only the style but also the spirit of tomb decoration changed and took a somber turn. Gaiety gave way to gloom and confidence to doubt. The Old and Middle Kingdom tomb decoration had focused primarily on scenes from daily life—work, games and public ceremonies —that were bright and cheerful. Toward the end of the 19th Dynasty the Osiris cult shifted the emphasis from life to death: to the funeral banquet, the preparation of the mummy and the judgment of the soul before Osiris.

The Middle Kingdom saw an increased use of painting as a major art medium. Simple painting of geometric designs and a few elementary colors had been known in prehistoric times, when paint was used to decorate stone and earthen vessels. In the First and Second Dynasties the Egyptians used paint to adorn the plastered mud-brick walls of their tombs with geometric patterns and some

At first the Egyptian artists approached the medium of paint timidly, using it merely to adorn the relief sculpture in solid color, or to render figures only in silhouettes. After a while they learned to paint with increasing vigor and movement. Tradition dictated that the high and mighty occupants of the tomb be treated in orthodox fashion, as with their statues. But this limitation did not apply to other subjects, so dancers, musicians, serving girls, animals, foreigners and captured enemies were often depicted in action. The range of subjects for painting expanded considerably in time: to the Old Kingdom's repertory of hunting scenes, fowling, work in the fields, dancing, games and funerary arrangements, the tomb painters of the New Kingdom added a civic note by showing important officials in the performance of their duties: receiving foreign emissaries, collecting taxes and participating in court ceremonies.

During the time of Amenhotep III, new thought was entering religion, literature and art. An increasing acquaintance with foreign cultures, resulting from Egypt's conquests under Thutmose III a generation before, plus the presence of many foreigners at the capital in Thebes, led to some erosion of the conservative and restricted Egyptian outlook. Eventually this erupted into revolution—the revolution of Akhenaton, the heretical Pharaoh who tried to make as radical a change in Egyptian religion, and failed.

Although change had been on the way, it had been coming slowly and gradually; now it leaped forward with sharp abruptness under the stimulus of the King. An inscription on a rock at Aswan says that Bak, Akhenaton's chief sculptor, was taught his craft by His Majesty himself. And if Akhenaton was unrealistic in his grasp of human nature and misread his people's readiness to overthrow their old religion, he had, oddly enough, an eye for accurate representation in art. Egyptian art

FURNITURE AND JEWELRY DESIGN *were two minor arts at which Egyptian craftsmen excelled. The intricately carved chair of boxwood and ebony is adorned with a figure of the god Bes flanked by symbols of other deities. The falcons on the 12th Dynasty collar are covered with gold leaf; the beads are turquoise, faïence and carnelian.*

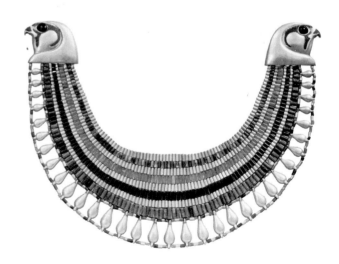

had earlier seen some foreshadowings of an incipient naturalism—the increased use of painting in the tombs had been accompanied by more attention to the details of how things look in nature, and statues had come to be rendered in slightly slackened poses. The revolutionary Akhenaton tried to transform the canons of art as he did the tenets of religion.

No artist's subject was ever better fitted for naturalistic treatment than Akhenaton himself, for he was a strange-looking man with a scrawny neck, a pear-shaped torso, thin, unmuscular legs, and a soft, sensitive mouth. In relief he had his artists show him with his family munching on a bone at table or dandling one of his infant daughters on his knee. Scenes of such emotional content had never before appeared in Egyptian art. The subject had always been shown in some more or less conventional pose.

In painting, the effect of the new artistic expression was even more dramatic. Besides introducing more naturalism than ever before, the artists made new use of space: walls were given over to whole scenes instead of being ruled off in registers, some of the representations continued from one wall to the next, and figures were integrated with rudimentary backgrounds of architecture and landscape.

Though Akhenaton's revolution in religion ended abruptly with his death, what he had started in art lingered on for a time. The same factor that kept the people from following his orders in religion enabled them to grasp and make something of the new movement in art. They were beginning to experience religion in a personal way and to grope for personal expression, but Akhenaton shut off that path by reserving to himself the worship of his god, the Aton, and by requiring the people to worship him. When he was gone, they returned to their old gods; but to a certain extent they al-

lowed the artists the opportunity to portray what they saw around them with the tools provided by the new naturalism. Some of the finest creations of the so-called Amarna style (named after the site of Akhenaton's new capital) are the reliefs in the tomb of Haremhab, an army general who took the throne at the end of the 18th Dynasty.

By the time of the second Ramses, a little over half a century after Akhenaton, art had taken another shift. By this time Egyptian civilization had reached its crest, though the Egyptians could hardly know it. They were still winning territories abroad, wealth was pouring into the national coffers, and the Egyptian spirit was expansive. This expansiveness produced the grandiose statues and tombs, and it also prompted the Egyptians to record in words and pictures the significant historical events of their era. Nevertheless, another spirit was emerging, one that cherished the achievements of the past and discouraged exploration and innovation.

Now when they carved statues and painted tomb pictures, the Egyptians turned to the works of their forebears for inspiration. Particularly as the country fell on troubled times, its people sought refuge from the present by gazing longingly at their history.

Once this reversion began, Egyptian art became progressively more imitative and uninspired, and as it did it got progressively more rigid. It was to remain imitative of the past for the rest of the nation's history.

Yet the craftsmanship of Egyptian artists never weakened. Egypt excelled also in the minor arts, where craftsmanship is of paramount importance. Archeologists have unearthed a vast wealth of objects testifying to the skill of Egyptian jewelers, leatherworkers, cabinetmakers, weavers and potters. Some of these minor Egyptian arts deserve special mention.

The first is the fashioning of stone vessels, an art that was known to the Neolithic Age and brought to new heights in the era of the Old Kingdom. Tombs of that period have yielded thousands of vases and bowls, made chiefly from limestone, alabaster and basalt, but also from the hardest stones—diorite, obsidian, flint and quartz. Incredible time and effort must have been required to shape and polish such resistant materials with the primitive tools available to the Egyptians. Some of their techniques remain mysteries. In one-piece, narrow-necked vases, for example, once the neck had been drilled through, how was the belly hollowed out? The skill the Egyptians acquired with small stone articles was the basis of their later mastery of gigantic stone blocks.

Another minor art in which Egyptian craftsmen excelled was faïence, but Egyptian faïence was made with a paste of powdered quartz rather than with clay and was coated with a vitreous paste. When fired it took on a beautiful glasslike shine. The earliest examples are all in blue; with experience the Egyptians learned to create green, white, black, violet, red, yellow and even multicolored effects. The objects they fashioned ranged from tiny beads to statues of moderate size, but vases, tiles and figurines were the most common.

Jewelry-making was also an important minor art in Egypt. Gold was plentiful, and so were agate, jasper, carnelian, garnet, amethyst and turquoise, which the Egyptians highly valued. Jewelers had reached by the time of the 12th Dynasty a level of skill that has never been exceeded. They made magnificent necklaces, bracelets and crowns, inlaying gold in the stones and interlacing strands of gold wire; and they fashioned clasps that fitted together with neat precision and looked like lotuses and cowrie shells. They made equally delicate boxes to hold these luxuries—some of ivory, some of wood, and many encrusted with gold.

Though the Egyptians had no good timber and imported most of what they used from Lebanon and Syria, their achievement in woodworking was noteworthy, and it has survived because of the country's dry climate. Wood is a perishable substance, and few wooden works of antiquity made in damper regions have lasted. Egyptian cabinetmakers mastered the medium as early as the First Dynasty, and exquisite specimens of canopies, beds, carrying-chairs, chariots, coffins, cosmetics boxes and ornaments have been found in the tombs of all periods, attesting to the remarkable skill of the Egyptian craftsman at joinery and veneering; at inlaying with faïence, ivory and semiprecious stones; and at overlaying with molded gold, silver and copper.

Taken in its entirety, ancient Egypt's artistic contribution was enormous. Egypt gave the world the first architecture entirely in stone, which for centuries was a model and inspiration for other nations. It is too much to suppose that later civilizations learned of the column and the architrave from Egypt; the idea of supporting a beam with upright posts is simple enough to have suggested itself to any people. The fact remains that the Egyptians were the first to do so. Many scholars believe that Greek sculptors of the Seventh and Sixth Centuries B.C. went to Egypt to learn the art of carving stone. Their creations developed into the sculpture of the great Periclean Age in the Fifth Century B.C., which subsequently exercised a pervasive influence on Western art.

But the greatness of Egyptian art does not depend on its influence on that of other nations. It lies in the quality and durability of the art itself: the massive symmetry of the pyramids, the sophistication of the sculpture, and the charm of the paintings and reliefs. The Egyptians created for eternity, and nothing that man has fashioned has proved more lasting than their great works of art.

FUNERAL BARGES *make up a royal cortege as the dead Pharaoh is borne up a canal from the Nile toward his Great Pyramid.*

THE PYRAMID BUILDERS

As soon as a pharaoh of the Old Kingdom came to power, he began planning the pyramid that would be his tomb. The great bureaucracy of builders and architects was set in motion. Each village sent its quota of laborers to the quarries or the construction site, and royal storehouses issued tools and clothing. They faced a colossal chore. The Great Pyramid built for Khufu at Gizeh was constructed of more than two million stone blocks, most weighing about two and a half tons. Despite the magnitude of the task, it was completed within the Pharaoh's 23-year reign in about 2600 B.C.—by men working with the simplest implements, without draft animals or even the wheel. They had to be inventive engineers, and some of the methods modern experts think they used are re-created here, in drawings showing the pyramid builders at their monumental work.

THE ARDUOUS WORK
OF THE QUARRIES

The Great Pyramid at Gizeh was built mostly of limestone. But some of the blocks were granite, and they posed serious problems. Granite is so hard that the Egyptians' copper chisels and saws could scarcely make a dent in it. Special dolerite hammers had to be used to chip rough gutters, or slots, in quarry walls; workers then fitted wooden wedges into the slots; soaked with water, the wood expanded and split off chunks of rock. The massive stone chunks were then hammered into rough blocks.

The blocks were painted with a variety of quarry marks. Some of the marks indicated the blocks' destination; others cautioned, "This side up." Still others gave the name of the quarry gang, such as the "Vigorous Gang," or the "Enduring Gang." Some carefree crews inscribed the daring message: "How drunk is the King!"

A QUARRY GANG (below) puts the last touches to stone blocks. Workmen at rear measure a surface and chip away rough spots; others (foreground) temper their copper tools. At left rear, a quarry mark is painted on.

TIPPING A BLOCK, *a team of quarry workers at Aswan (above, right) eases the stone onto log rollers. Whichever surface of the granite block was to be moved face down was finished beforehand so it would slide smoothly to the ramp at far left.*

AT RAMP'S END, *workmen load a granite block onto a wooden sledge. By using rollers, ramps and sledges, work gangs were able to haul blocks weighing up to 15 tons from the quarry to barges waiting along the Nile hundreds of yards away.*

THE FOUNDATIONS OF A TOMB

Khufu's architects, planning their Pharaoh's enormous pyramid—still the largest stone structure in the world—had first to choose an appropriate site in the desert. As a rough substructure for the tomb, they chose a rocky knoll rising above the surrounding desert floor. Surveyors then marked out the site so that the pyramid's base would form a perfect square.

With that accomplished, the architects directed work gangs to cut steplike terraces into the irregular sides of the hill. These terraces, which would serve as the foundation on which all the stone blocks were laid, had to be absolutely level if the entire structure was not to be askew. To assure this level foundation the pyramid builders erected an extensive system of water-filled trenches about its base. Then, using the water level as a standard, they were able to lay out the 13-acre site so evenly that experts using modern instruments have found that the southeast corner of the pyramid stands only half an inch higher than the northwest corner.

TERRACING THE HILL (above), workers use levers to dislodge blocks while others, at right, drag rocks away on sledges. In the foreground men carry water in clay pots to fill the connecting ditches which gave builders a standard level on all sides of the pyramid.

STONECUTTERS (left) chip away at the rocky ground to level a terrace. Squatting surveyors set a level, using taut strings tied to sticks dipped into the water trenches. From these strings, workmen with rods determine how deep the stonecutters must go.

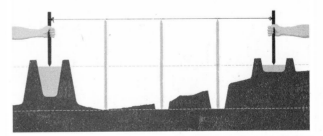

SETTING A LEVEL by means of connected water trenches is illustrated in this diagram. A string is stretched between two sticks of equal length, held touching the water. The ground is then leveled until measuring rods (center) show the floor is parallel to the string.

TOILING THOUSANDS ON A
MONUMENTAL CONSTRUCTION JOB

The Greek historian Herodotus, taken in by the tall tales of local guides, reported that 100,000 slaves had worked on the Great Pyramid. The fact is that only about 4,000 construction workers were used at a time and they were free citizens drafted for the public work. Laborers worked in gangs of 18 or 20 men, hauling the heavy stone blocks up ramps and setting them in place. Finally, from the 481-foot apex, masons cut down the blocks to form the smooth, sloping sides of the pyramid. Despite the great labor, some gangs were so pleased to work for the King that, as a later foreman said, they toiled "without a single man getting exhausted, without a man thirsting," and at last "came home in good spirits, sated with bread, drunk with beer, as if it were the beautiful festival of a god."

RISING RAMPS *were built in tiers along the four sides of the pyramid, three to go up and one to go down. Each ramp began at one corner (outer arrows) and all ended at the topmost level of construction (inner arrows). The brown outline shows the path of one ramp.*

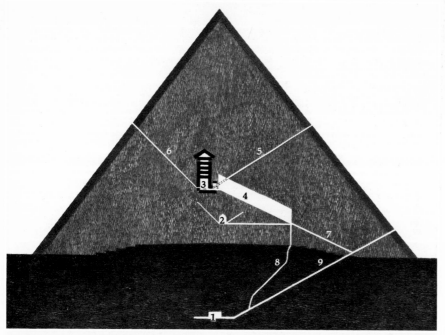

THE INNER DESIGN *of the pyramid included two burial chambers (1 and 2) which were left incomplete. The final chamber (3) was reached through the Grand Gallery (4) and was ventilated by two narrow air shafts (5 and 6). After the Ascending Corridor (7) was sealed from within by stone plugs, workmen in the Gallery escaped down a shaft (8) and up the Descending Corridor (9).*

THE KING'S CHAMBER *was roofed with enormous granite slabs that formed five stress-relieving compartments. Now, though many slabs have cracked, the roofing remains firm.*

THE INTRICATE INTERIOR
OF THE TOMB

For its outward size alone the Great Pyramid was called one of the Seven Wonders of the Ancient World. But the interior, with its corridors, passageways, air shafts, Grand Gallery and King's Chamber, is no less an architectural marvel. The Egyptians demonstrated outstanding engineering skill in designing these interior structures to withstand the massive weight of stone above them. The Grand Gallery, for example, was built with a tiered, braced ceiling; the King's Chamber was designed with six roofs to displace the weight of the blocks overhead. Originally, Khufu had planned a somewhat smaller pyramid with his burial chamber sunk deep into bedrock below the base. But as his aspirations grew, he twice enlarged the tomb's plan and each time ordered the burial chamber to be raised higher up in the pyramid.

THE GRAND GALLERY, *a sloping room 153 feet long and 28 feet high, was built with stone sealing plugs (black) already inside. When workmen on the side ramp (shaded) removed restraining crossbeams, the plugs slid down to seal the Ascending Corridor.*

SEALING THE TOMB, workmen ease stone blocks down the Grand Gallery into the Ascending Corridor. They work with ropes stretched over beams set in grooves in the walls. Once the Ascending Corridor was sealed, workmen blocked the other passages (including the tomb's entrance) with stone slabs. These extraordinary measures foiled even the most ingenious tomb robbers for at least 400 years. Finally, however, the pyramid was broken into, and the mummy and funerary treasures were taken.

FINAL PROCESSION
TO THE OTHER WORLD

When Khufu died at his palace, his body was borne across the Nile to Gizeh, where the pyramid stood ready, surrounded by a complex of lesser buildings. The King's body was prepared for burial in the Valley Temple, south of the monument. On the day of burial, priests led the way up the Great Causeway as workmen, shown below, towed a fu-

A GREAT CAUSEWAY, *little of which is intact today, led to a rectangular mortuary temple in front of the Great Pyramid. From there the coffin was taken to a spot below the tomb entrance and then hauled up about 56 feet to the opening.*

nerary bark bearing the King's mummiform coffin. Others came behind bearing a boat ready for sailing in the afterworld; such boats were buried in pits beside the pyramid. One worker *(right foreground)* falls prostrate before the approaching coffin. In the immediate vicinity of the pyramid were several small villages, inhabited by the priests and workmen charged with maintaining the vast burial grounds as a resting place for the dead Pharaoh. Yet his spirit was thought to dwell there only periodically. As a pyramid hymn records: "He is no longer upon earth, he is in the sky! He rushes at the sky like a heron; he has kissed the sky like a falcon; he has leapt skyward like a grasshopper."

7
WORKS OF THE MIND

Two steps mark the end of a people's infancy: the devising of abstract tools to deal with the world around them, and the creation of symbols to record their ideas. The Egyptians were among the earliest peoples to take these steps. They fashioned a simple arithmetic and with it measured their fields, estimated yields of grain, and provided for feeding their armies of citizens. They observed the heavens and learned to know the movements of some of the stars. They studied human anatomy, and learned to deal with sickness and accident. Above all, they learned to record their ideas, and with the craft of writing they left a record of their achievements, a good many of which they transmitted to the rest of the world.

The invention of writing took place toward the end of the Fourth Millennium B.C., first in Mesopotamia and shortly afterward in Egypt. Egypt probably acted under the spur of Mesopotamia's example. In both Mesopotamia and Egypt, writing developed from pictorial symbols. Mesopotamia quickly transformed the pictures into the wedge-shaped strokes that are called cuneiform—from *cuneus*, the Latin for "wedge." Not so Egypt. The first form of Egyptian writing was the hieroglyphic (a miniature picture) and the Egyptians never abandoned it. From its origin about the time of the First Dynasty to its last recorded appearance in an inscription dated 394 A.D. on the Temple of Isis at Philae, it remained a combination of ideograms (signs standing for ideas) and phonograms (signs standing for sounds). The name "hieroglyph" comes from the Greek and means "sacred carvings"—probably because Greek travelers first saw such writing on the walls of temples.

Originally each hieroglyph stood for a whole word or idea. But as hieroglyphic writing developed, most of the signs took on phonetic values. They could be used to stand for sounds and, along with other hieroglyphs, to spell out words that had nothing to do with what the pictures portrayed—much as if we were to spell the word "beagle" by combining a picture of a bee with one of an eagle. The Egyptians, by selecting 24 hieroglyphs for 24 different consonant sounds and adding others to represent clusters of consonants, approached an alphabet; but, lacking vowels, they never took the final step to alphabetical writing. Instead they mingled the hieroglyphs that stood for sounds with the others that stood for ideas.

The hieroglyphs were perfectly satisfactory so long as most writing was incised in stone. But when it occurred to the Egyptians to use other writing materials, they developed two additional, more flowing scripts from the hieroglyphs. The first, the hieratic, or "priestly," writing, which is almost as old as the hieroglyphic, is a simplified form of hieroglyphic, suitable for rapid writing with a brush on wood or with a reed pen on papyrus. Its name is misleading, for it was used for secular as well as religious purposes. The second kind of Egyptian writing, the demotic, or "popular," form, is a further cursive refinement of the hieratic. It was developed quite late, about 700 B.C., mainly for secular matters such as letters, accounts and records. Like the hieratic, it was written chiefly on papyrus.

Inscriptions on the walls of temples, tombs and monuments have preserved a good many of the historical records, biographies, incantations and prayers that the Egyptians recorded with their writing. These, however, are usually abbreviated. Most of what is known of Egypt's literature proper comes from papyrus rolls, which have survived the centuries thanks to Egypt's dry climate. The Egyptians wrote on them with lampblack. Very few papyri have escaped damage and many have faded with age, but some of those that remain can be read as easily today as when they were inscribed.

In evaluating Egyptian literature, it must always be borne in mind that there is little by which to judge. Moreover, the Egyptian mode of expression is so vastly different from that of English that the veil of translation it must wear is exceptionally heavy. Finally, much of the writing was done in the language of the Old Kingdom long after that period had passed—which would be somewhat like having English literature of the present day written in the archaic 14th Century language of Chaucer.

Akhenaton's revolution, though it had no lasting effect on religion, left a mark on literature. Though texts from his period onward continued to be written chiefly in classical Egyptian, the vernacular had begun to creep in. As a result, it comes out rather better in translation than does literature from the earlier periods.

In Egyptian prose, where less is generally lost in translation than is lost in poetry, the bulk of what survives consists of accounts of Creation, stories of the doings of the gods, collections of wise sayings and observations on the state of the world. It has no great literary distinction, but it throws precious light on the thought of the times.

Two works that have for the latter reason received a good deal of attention are *The Protests of the Eloquent Peasant* and *The Admonitions of Ipuwer*. Both were probably written during the troubled age between the Old and the Middle Kingdoms. The protesting peasant had been robbed by someone with court connections and complained to the Chief Steward of the Palace. The steward, captivated by the peasant's eloquence, listened while the peasant made nine appeals, and then restored his stolen property. The significance of the story lies in the freedom of speech granted to the lowly peasant and in the fact that the robber, a man higher-born than he, was required to make restitution. It indicates an awakening of social justice, an idea inconceivable in Old Kingdom times.

The Admonitions of Ipuwer is the work of a sage who took a poor view of just about everything. He mourned the passing of the old ways, and he made bold to reprove the pharaoh for his failure to keep order. The pharaoh, he wrote, is "the herdsman of all men. . . . Authority, Perception, and Justice are with thee, but it is confusion which thou wouldst set throughout the land." Like *The Protests of the Eloquent Peasant*, this work reflects a democratic

PAPYRUS REEDS

PEELING THE RIND   SLICING STRIPS

THE PAPYRUS REED, *shown above at left, was the raw material of Egyptian papermaking. The Egyptians are thought to have used papyrus documents as early as the First Dynasty. The reeds were also used to make such necessities as sails, rope and sandals. The first step in making paper was to cut the 7-to-10-foot stems into shorter pieces. Then the rind was removed and the exposed inner pith was sliced lengthwise into thin strips, as illustrated above.*

COVER CLOTH

FLAT STONE

POLISHING STONE

POUNDING MALLET

FORMING PAPER *from the raw papyrus, the Egyptians laid strips crosswise in a double layer on a flat stone. A cloth was laid over the strips and the papyrus was beaten with a wooden mallet for an hour or two—until the strips were matted together in a single sheet. This sheet was then pressed out under a heavy weight. Finally a papermaker polished the sheet with a rounded stone, trimmed the edges and pasted several sheets end-to-end into a long roll.*

spirit. It would not have occurred to anyone during the Old Kingdom to quarrel with the pharaoh.

The kind of prose in which Egypt's authors come off best is narrative. *The Tale of the Two Brothers,* which was written toward the end of the New Kingdom, begins promisingly as an Egyptian parallel to the Biblical story of Potiphar and Joseph. In the Egyptian version the older brother's wife tries without success to seduce the younger brother, Bata. As in the Bible story, the innocent man is punished through the accusations of the scorned woman. After a swift and spicy start, however, the narrative wanders into a hodgepodge of mythological fantasy that one would have to be Egyptian to appreciate.

The field of historical romance is somewhat better. A contribution of the Middle Kingdom, *The Story of Sinuhe,* is not so full of fantasy; among its virtues are its convincing reflection of the political climate of the 12th Dynasty and its portrayal of the Egyptian's affectionate loyalty to his homeland. It tells how Sinuhe, a highly placed courtier, fled the country after the pharaoh had been attacked by conspirators and died. Probably Sinuhe had not been among the assassins, but he left anyhow; he made his way to Syria and flourished mightily there. Yet he was unhappy, for like all Egyptians he regarded Egypt as the only place worth living in, and when in his old age he was permitted by the new pharaoh to return to Egypt, he looked forward with ecstatic joy to the bliss of Egyptian burial. There are some good touches—for example, a lively description of Sinuhe's reception at court and of his relief when he discards his heavy Syrian clothes for the cool comfort of Egyptian linen.

From the period right after the decline of the New Kingdom comes a unique narrative whose quality few will question: *The Voyage of Wenamon.* The work has convincing character portrayal, a fast-moving plot and a verisimilitude that vividly brings the world of the 12th Century B.C.

to life. It is the tale, told in the first person, of the trials and tribulations of a comically self-important priest who is sent to Syria to purchase cedar logs for the divine boat of the god Amon Re. Though Egypt was by then no longer a first-rate power, Wenamon behaved as if he was back in the great days of Thutmose III. The poor fellow's troubles began when his ship first put into a Palestinian port and he was robbed. After extricating himself from this predicament by the simple expedient of robbing someone else, he went steadily from bad to worse. He had a humiliating interview with the Prince of Byblos, who had lumber for sale; had to cool his heels for months until his employer forwarded the payment that the flint-hearted seller insisted on having before delivery; then left with his precious cargo and eluded a pack of sailors who were demanding retribution for his theft, only to be shipwrecked on Cyprus. At this tantalizing point, the papyrus on which the tale is told breaks off.

A favorite genre in Egyptian letters, popular during all periods, was "wisdom literature"—words of advice by an elderly sage to the young. In the Old Kingdom the comments were all worldly and pragmatic. By the time of the Middle Kingdom, the tone of the wisdom literature had changed. The *Instruction for King Merikare* has advice for the new monarch that reveals an enlightened view of a ruler's responsibility and intimates that a man should be honored for his ability rather than for his birth. The most fascinating work of this genre is the relatively late *Instruction of Amenemopet*, which was written sometime in the post-empire period. It counsels humility and resignation, attitudes that developed after the New Kingdom had

declined and Egyptian self-confidence had waned. Sections of it so closely parallel parts of the Book of Proverbs of the Old Testament that a relation between the two is beyond doubt. Amenemopet begins with the words: "Give thy ears, hear what is said, / Give thy heart to understand them." The corresponding lines in Proverbs (xxii. 17) read: "Incline thine ear and hear my words, / And apply thine heart to apprehend." Proverbs xxii. 18 continues: "For it is pleasant if thou keep them in thy belly, / That they may be fixed like a peg upon thy lips." These words parallel Amenemopet's: "To put them in thy heart is worth while . . . / Let them rest in the casket of thy belly . . . / They shall be a mooring-stake for thy tongue."

Many more such parallels could be cited. In the First Millennium B.C., relations between Palestine and Egypt were close, with traffic flowing ceaselessly between the two, so there was frequent cultural interchange. A few scholars have argued that the Hebrew influenced the Egyptian, but the great majority put it the other way around, and indeed see Egyptian influence on many other portions of the Old Testament as well.

Some of Egypt's finest writing is in the field of lyric poetry. The sophisticated New Kingdom produced love poetry of genuine charm and feeling. Here is the lyrical longing of a lover who for a full week has been denied the sight of his beloved, whom he calls his "sister."

Seven days to yesterday I have not seen the
*   sister,*
*   And a sickness has invaded me.*
My body has become heavy,

Forgetful of my own self.
If the chief of physicians come to me,
 My heart is not content with their remedies;
The lector priests, no way out is in them:—
 My sickness will not be probed.

To say to me: "Here she is!" is what will
 revive me;
 Her name is what will lift me up;
The going in and out of her messengers
 Is what will revive my heart.
More beneficial to me is the sister than any
 remedies;
 She is more to me than the collected
 writings.
My health is her coming in from outside:
 When I see her, then I am well.
If she opens her eye, my body is young again;
 If she speaks, then I am strong again;
When I embrace her, she drives evil away
 from me—
 But she has gone forth from me for seven
 days!

Here are a few stanzas from Akhenaton's "Hymn to the Aton," fervid and noble lines that reveal the heights to which Egyptian lyric poetry could rise:

All beasts are content with their pasturage;
Trees and plants are flourishing.
The birds which fly from their nests,
Their wings are stretched out in praise to thee.
All beasts spring upon their feet.
Whatever flies and alights,
They live when thou hast risen for them.

The ships are sailing north and south as well,
For every way is open at thy appearance.
The fish in the river dart before thy face;
Thy rays are in the midst of the great green sea.

How manifold it is, what thou hast made!
They are hidden from the face of man.
O sole god, like whom there is no other!
Thou didst create the world according to thy desire,
Whilst thou wert alone:
All men, cattle and wild beasts,
Whatever is on earth, going upon its feet,
And what is on high, flying with its wings.

As has often been pointed out, these verses are close in spirit to the 104th Psalm.

In about the same era when they were developing hieroglyphic writing, the Egyptians were exploring engineering, astronomy and other abstract disciplines. Their achievements are the more remarkable because their methods were rudimentary. To begin with, they used simple arithmetic rather than higher mathematics, and even their arithmetic was limited to addition and subtraction, which they used variously to perform the processes of multiplication and division. To multiply 23 by 13, they first doubled and redoubled the multiplicand, 23, as follows:

```
*   1    23
    2    46
*   4    92
*   8   184
```

They stopped when they had as many doublings as would add up to 13, the multiplier (8+ 4+ 1; the numbers starred). Next they added the corresponding numbers on the right $(184+92+23)$ to arrive at the result, 299.

They used a similar system for dividing. To divide 49 by 8 they doubled the divisor:

	1	8
*	2	16
*	4	32
	8	64

Then, by trial and error, they determined that the doublings $4+2$ added up to 48, the number closest to the figure to be divided, and thus arrived at the answer of $6\frac{1}{8}$. The fraction was the most serious handicap to their arithmetical computation, for the Egyptians used only unit fractions—fractions with a numerator of 1. What is today expressed simply with the figure $\frac{13}{16}$, they expressed as $\frac{1}{2}+\frac{1}{4}+\frac{1}{16}$.

Though in doubling numbers ad infinitum the Egyptians were in fact multiplying, and though with their unit fractions they were in fact dealing with the parts of a whole, they never seem to have grasped the fundamental principles underlying the procedures and the simple way to handle them.

The reason they did not go further was that they were a pragmatic people, interested in numbers solely for practical purposes, not for any abstract reasons. They had to learn how to measure the areas of their fields, to gauge the rise of the Nile, to estimate supplies for work gangs and armies. They managed, in spite of their rudimentary arithmetical processes and cumbersome system of numerical notation, to devise ways to determine the area of triangles and rectangles and other figures, to compute elementary volumes (including that of a truncated pyramid), even to arrive at the relatively accurate figure of 3.16 for π. The pyramids were so accurately laid out that they depart but a fraction of an inch from a true square (which may be as much a testament to the Egyptians' patience as it is to their skill).

As observers of heavenly bodies the Egyptians reveal the same painstaking attention as in their engineering. They charted the heavens, identified many of the fixed stars and devised instruments to calculate the movements of others. When they laid the foundation of a temple or monument, they determined the axis by the stars; the Great Pyramid at Gizeh is so aligned that its slopes face the cardinal points of the compass almost exactly.

Despite their limited system of computation and their primitive fractional notation, the Egyptians made two contributions of fundamental importance to posterity. The first was the solar calendar of 365 days. The Babylonians, who were considerably further advanced in astronomy than the Egyptians, retained a highly unsatisfactory calendar based on the moon. So did the mathematically minded Greeks. As late as the Fifth Century B.C., during the Golden Age of Athens, when Aeschylus and Sophocles were writing masterpieces of literary form and harmony, the calendar they lived by was primitive. The Egyptians, however, even as early as the Third Millennium B.C., had worked out a feasible calendar. It was based on the sun and had 12 thirty-day months plus five additional days. They arrived at this calendar by observing the behavior of Sirius, the brightest star in the heavens. Once a year Sirius rises on the eastern horizon a moment or two before dawn. The Egyptians noted that this occurrence seemed to herald the eagerly awaited annual flood of the Nile, and they fixed this moment as the beginning of their calendar year.

In the First Century B.C., when Julius Caesar decided to improve the lunar calendar in use in Rome in his day, he assigned the task of devising a new one to an astronomer from Alexandria. The scholar worked out an adaptation of the Egyptian calendar; and the Julian calendar, used in the West for 16 centuries thereafter, came into being.

The second important contribution the Egyptians made by their observations of the heavens was the

SEATED SCRIBE *looks up from his work in this Old Kingdom sculpture, one and a half feet high. As keepers of all records, scribes held an important place in Egyptian life and were well aware of their power. One boasted, "It is the scribe who imposes taxes . . . who commands the whole country." Another urged the young to "be a scribe . . . more effective is a book than a decorated tombstone."*

division of day and night into 12 segments each. A segment represented $\frac{1}{12}$ of the time between sunrise and sunset or between sunset and sunrise, so the length of an hour varied with the seasons. The Egyptians measured the passage of the hours by means of a stone bowl with an aperture at the bottom, through which water escaped at a fixed rate. The bowl had different marks to indicate the hour at different seasons of the year. The Egyptian water clock, or a variation of it, remained the most efficient timepiece until the invention of the mechanical clock in medieval Europe made popular the standard hour.

If the Egyptians were behind the Babylonians in mathematics and astronomy, they were far ahead in a branch of learning that had a special appeal for a people of a practical turn of mind—medicine.

In the ancient Near East there was no sharp line between medicine and religion. Disease was believed to be the work of the gods, indicating the presence in the body of evil spirits or of poisons the spirits had injected, and cure meant cleansing the body of such intrusions. As spirits were thought to behave like people, treatment included warnings, threats, curses and orders accompanied by the appropriate gestures; using exactly the proper gestures was considered to be of utmost importance.

Treatment could also involve putting concoctions into the body through any of its openings—ears, nose, anus, but above all the mouth. Since the prime purpose of the recipes was to rid the body of unwelcome spirits, they often took an unappetizing form. Many consisted of a miscellany of substances calculated to turn the stomach even of a demon. An Egyptian doctor was in effect both priest and magician, adept both at concocting drugs and at uttering incantations against evil spirits.

Nevertheless, there were doctors in Egypt who practiced real medicine even by modern definition —the first in the world's history. A good part of the proof comes from the Edwin Smith Surgical Papyrus, which is named for the American Egyptologist who acquired it. The document is a milestone in the history of medicine. It is a medical textbook, and it deals with its subject in a rational fashion. The subject is the treatment of physical injuries (and this is doubtless one reason magic and mumbo jumbo play almost no part in it: there is no mystery about the cause of such ailments).

The papyrus takes up 48 cases of injury—wounds, fractures, dislocations—in a systematic order, starting from the head and working downward: 10 cases of injury to the brain, four to the nose, and so on to the spinal column. In each case the condition is carefully described, and the descriptions make abundantly clear that an examination by an Egyptian doctor was a thorough business. It included interrogation, inspection and functional tests such as having the patient walk or move his limbs to determine the area of injury. Then followed a diagnosis and one of three conclusions: "an ailment which I will treat," "an ailment with which I will contend," "an ailment not to be treated"—in other words: favorable, uncertain, unfavorable.

Treatment recommended in the papyrus included reducing dislocations, healing fractures by the use of splints and casts, and bringing open wounds together with sutures, clamps or a kind of adhesive plaster. Mummies reveal numerous examples of fractures that healed without complication. What is striking is the levelheaded approach of the handbook; it reveals a point of view that in some aspects differs little from that of modern medicine.

A second medical work, only slightly less impressive, is the Ebers Medical Papyrus. Unlike the Edwin Smith Surgical Papyrus, it is not a monograph on a single subject, but rather a teaching manual for general practitioners. It has a surgical section in the manner of the Edwin Smith Papyrus; a section on the heart and its vessels, which is a most interesting essay on speculative medical philosophy; and another on pharmacy. One of its remedies is a prescription for castor oil as a laxative.

Herodotus declared that Egypt's doctors were highly specialized, and this has sometimes been taken as an indication of the level Egyptian medicine reached. Quite the contrary—specialization is a well-established feature of primitive medicine; the medicine man frequently limited his practice to certain areas or problems only. The Egyptian doctor's fame rests on what the medical papyri have revealed—the unquestioned presence of a rational attitude toward the aspects of medicine which an ancient Egyptian could deal with practically.

In their own day the reputation of Egypt's doctors reached far beyond the Nile Valley. They were the ancient world's equivalent of the Viennese psychoanalysts. The clay tablets found at Tell el Amarna indicate that Egyptian physicians were frequently sent to foreign courts in Syria and Assyria, and the kings of Persia are known to have employed Egyptian doctors. And the Egyptians' herbal prescriptions and some of their treatments were so highly prized that they spread throughout the whole of the Mediterranean area.

Egyptian medicine is at the roots of modern Western medicine. The Egyptian calendar is the basis of the modern Western calendar, for the latter is but an improved version of the Julian calendar. It is even possible that the hieroglyphs inspired the Phoenician alphabet, which is indirectly the prototype of the modern Latin alphabet.

If the Egyptians were not a scientific people in the modern sense or in the Greek sense, nor speculative in their literature; if they were simply a pragmatic people who met their practical needs without reflecting on the meaning of what they did or why, their achievements are nonetheless creditable—if only because they comprised the first steps out of civilization's infancy.

HIEROGLYPHIC PRAISE *to Sesostris I, at Karnak, includes his royal name in a frame, or cartouche.*

THE MESSAGE OF THE STONES

For almost 15 centuries, men gazed fascinated upon Egyptian hieroglyphics without comprehending their meaning. The last men who actually used these signs were Egyptian priests of the Fourth Century A.D., and they were so secretive about the meaning that European scholars of the period—and thereafter —believed the hieroglyphics were mystical devices of some obscure sacred rite. But in 1822 a French linguist dramatically proved that the perched birds, staring faces and coiled snakes on the stones of Egypt could form words unrelated to their images. Only then did Western men begin to realize that an entire language lay before them, holding the key to what had hitherto been a land of mystery.

UNLOCKING A LOST LANGUAGE

The vital clue to hieroglyphic translation is a broken slab of black basalt, shown below, unearthed by French troops digging trenches near Rashid, or Rosetta, during Napoleon's Egyptian campaign of 1799. The proclamation carved on it, praising Ptolemy V in 196 B.C., is of relatively little significance; what is important is the fact that the inscription appears in two languages. Although scholars immediately understood the value of the Greek text in decoding the hieroglyphics, as well as an Egyptian script called demotic, 23 years passed before the Rosetta Stone finally surrendered its secret with the deciphering of a single word of hieroglyphics *(opposite)*.

THE DECIPHERER, *Jean François Champollion, was* *a brilliant linguist who worked from an 1808 copy* *of the Rosetta Stone's inscription. He labored on* *it for 14 years without ever seeing the stone itself.*

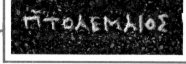

Ptolemy's name, which appears in the Rosetta Stone's Greek text as *Ptolemaios (bottom)*, was the first word recognized in hieroglyphics *(top)*. But early attempts to interpret its eight symbols were stymied by the traditional belief that all of the hieroglyphs could be translated as pictures of words. Even after an English scientist, Thomas Young, assigned sound values to several symbols, Champollion held to the belief that the lion symbolized the Greek word for war—*p(t)olemos*—anagrammed in the word *Ptolemaios.*

Champollion, finally deciding that Ptolemy might be read phonetically, patiently reconstructed the name, sound by sound, from Greek and Coptic into demotic, then into an earlier hieratic script and finally into hieroglyphics. It came out *p-t-o-l-m-y-s*, or Ptolmis, and could be spelled both right-to-left and in other directions, as on the obelisk at right.

In 1822 a copy of the inscription from an obelisk at Philae, excavated seven years earlier, was made available to Champollion. He was stunned to see confirmed in its hieroglyphics a name he had reconstructed many times from a demotic papyrus: the cartouche of Cleopatra.

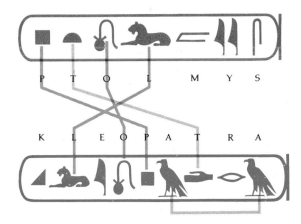

A comparison of two royal names from the Philae inscription—a tribute to the goddess Isis from Ptolemy IX and his wife Cleopatra, ancestors of the best-known Cleopatra—shows the deductive process by which Champollion confirmed that some hieroglyphics were meant to be heard as well as seen. Assuming the pronunciation would be similar to the Greek, he first identified three phonetic symbols—the *p*, *o* and *l* sounds—present in both names. Champollion correctly concluded that the two different *t* signs were homophones, like the *f* and *ph* in English: equally valid symbols for the same sound. Thus armed with four known letters, Champollion was able to deduce the missing ones from their positions.

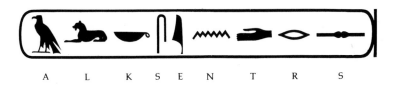

A L K S E N T R S

Now possessing a combined total of 12 phonograms, or sound symbols, Champollion eagerly applied them to a third cartouche and was able to decipher the name *a-l-k-s-e-n-t-r-s* —Alexander *(above)*. Convinced that his phonetic approach would work for all non-Egyptian names, Champollion gathered as many cartouches as he could find dating from the Ptolemaic and Roman periods and quickly transliterated 80, in the process increasing his list of known phonetic signs severalfold. The acid test came in September of 1822, when he tackled some cartouches predating the Greek and Roman eras, and achieved a tremendous breakthrough by deciphering his first purely Egyptian names: Ramses and Thutmose.

PICTURES THAT SPELL WORDS

Hieroglyphics may have begun in a prehistoric era as picture writing, like that found in Stone Age caves. As early Egyptians were confronted with an idea difficult to express in pictures, they probably devised a rebus to "spell" the desired word (like combining pictures of a bee and a leaf to show the word "belief" in English). Language experts can only guess at these beginnings, however, since the oldest surviving hieroglyphics—dating from around 3100 B.C.—represent a fully developed written language. Although Egyptians never evolved an alphabet as we know it, they set aside symbols for every consonant sound in their speech. The system proved remarkably efficient even though no attempt was made—except in the phonetic reproduction of foreign names—to symbolize vowels. By combining phonograms, or sound pictures, scribes could form a skeletonized version of any word.

	UNILITERALS		
SIGN	![owl]	![mouth]	![water]
OBJECT DEPICTED	Owl	Mouth	Water
APPROXIMATE SOUND	m	r	n

M + S + Ḥ = CROCODILE

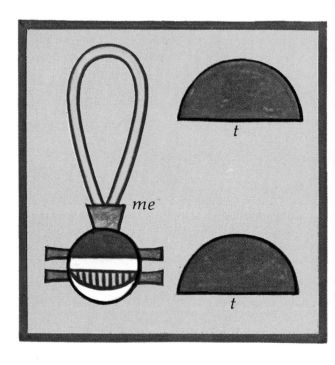

ME + T + T = LIKENESS

To express the three consonants of their word for crocodile —which may have been pronounced "meseh," "miseh" or even "emseh" after vowels were added—the Egyptians combined three single-consonant signs. They also might have added a purely visual symbol of a crocodile for emphasis.

Early decipherers might have translated a jug of milk and two loaves of bread as food symbols, but they would have been wrong, for these are sound values representing a word difficult to express in a picture. The first symbol is actually a double consonant, the e approximating a gulped sound.

SYMBOLS OF SOUNDS

The Egyptian "alphabet" consists of signs for 24 single-consonant sounds and a great number of two- and three-consonant combinations. The diagram below shows some of these "letters," the objects they once signified and approximations of their sounds as close as present knowledge and the limitations of the English alphabet permit.

					BILITERALS					TRILITERALS		
ail chick	Loaf	Bolt	Twisted flax		Face	Milk jug (in a net)	Goose	Swallow or martin		Beetle or scarab	Sandal strap	Heart and windpipe
w	t	s	ḥ		hr	me	sa	wr		kheper	ankh	nefer

WR + R = GREAT

An unusual feature of many words is the use of an extra sign, a phonetic complement, to assist the reader. The mouth symbol for *r* confirmed that the word ended with that sound. Phonetic complements were commonly added to words possessing the two- or three-consonant signs.

THE FLOW OF LANGUAGE

Egyptians were always conscious of the beauty as well as the practicality of their hieroglyphics, and often used them for their decorative effect. There was no spacing or punctuation to break the flow of words, which might be written either horizontally or vertically. The pictures of living creatures usually faced the starting point and the hieroglyphs were read from that direction, with the symbols on top always taking precedence over those below. Each group of signs was symmetrically arranged to fit into an invisible rectangle.

A PICTORIAL GLOSSARY

Not all hieroglyphs surrendered their old function as word pictures to become phonetic symbols. Of about 700 hieroglyphs commonly used during the New Kingdom, at least 100 remained strictly visual. Used at times to represent the words they depicted, more often they were tacked onto phonetic spellings of the same words as determinatives to provide guides. Thus the word for obelisk—*tekhen*—is usually shown as phonetic hieroglyphs forming the consonants t+kh+n, followed by the symbol of an obelisk.

Weep	Man, Son	Cattle, Ox	Beer pot, Drunkenness	Bee, Honey

Nestling	Jubilation	Sail upstream	Woman, Widow	Hill country, Desert

A FATHER'S TRIBUTE TO HIS SON

This sentence, which defies translation if its hieroglyphs are read for their visual meanings *(right)*, says: "It is my son who causes my name to live upon this stele." Taken from the 12th Dynasty epitaph of a military officer, it illustrates how phonetic hieroglyphs—with assists from two determinatives and a phonetic complement—could not only form words and phrases, but could convey emotion—the pride of a doting father in his son.

SOUND AND SIGHT

Because so many hieroglyphic words could be read as homonyms or near-homonyms—i.e., like-sounding words, such as the English *wait*, *weight* and *wade*—Egyptian scribes made liberal use of determinative symbols to be sure their readers grasped the correct meaning. The letters *hnw*, at top right, could be pronounced as anything from *hinew* to *ohanow* and could have a number of different meanings. Therefore the word is never seen without one of several determinatives: a beer jug to indicate the word for a liquid measure; a man giving the ritual sign of jubilation to show the word for rejoicing; and the figures of a man and woman over a plural symbol (three parallel strokes) to illustrate the word for neighbors or associates. By this system, the Egyptians could use the same grouping of letters to indicate as many as 10 completely different words.

1. *A reed leaf, plus . . .*
2. *water* = IT IS
3. *A goose, plus . . .*
4. *determinative man symbol* = (MY) SON
5. *Folded cloth, plus . . .*
6. *a sandal strap* = (WHO) CAUSES TO LIVE
7. *A mouth, plus . . .*
8. *water* = (MY) NAME
9. *A face over a line* = UPON
10. *A spindle, plus . . .*
11. *a quail chick (phonetic complement), plus . . .*
12. *determinative writing symbol (book roll)* = STELE
13. *A mat, plus . . .*
14. *water* = THIS

STRIKING SYMBOLS OF A PROUD TRADITION

Hieroglyphics were everywhere in ancient Egypt, sometimes simply incised in stone, but often glowing with brilliant color and occasionally covered with gold. They constituted the monumental language of Egypt for over 3,000 years, even though rarely used for ordinary writing after development of the hieratic and demotic scripts. The last known inscription dates to 394 A.D., when Egypt had long been a Roman province. By then so many hieroglyphs had been added to the language, their meanings deliberately obscured by the priestly scribes, that the signs were incomprehensible to most Egyptians. Not until the successors of Champollion had labored for another half century was the last vestige of their mystery swept away, and the beauty and clarity of hieroglyphics fully revealed.

GOLDEN FIGURES *adorn the funerary bed of Queen Hetephras.*

A VIVID CARTOUCHE *dominates a painting taken from Queen Nofretari's tomb.*

A WRITTEN FORM *of hieroglyphics appears in this portion of a funerary papyrus.*

PHONETIC SYMBOLS, *carved on a monument of Thutmose I at Karnak, display the formal grace and symmetry that characterize hieroglyphic art.*

8
CENTURIES OF DECLINE

For 2,000 years and more, the Egyptians had met and surmounted the crises of war, drought and famine. The civilization they had built seemed impervious to the assaults of time. But during the 20th Dynasty, a combination of factors—loss of empire, steady shrinkage of the pharaoh's prestige, and the impact of the Iron Age—signaled danger. The impressive achievements of 20 centuries of civilization were too solid to crumble under these blows, but an irrevocable process of decline had begun.

After 1100 B.C., Egypt's role as a great political power approached its end. Racked by internal dissension, the nation broke apart at its traditional geographic seam, and weak successors of the mighty pharaohs took over a land that henceforth would be frequently divided. At first, merchant princes from Tanis ruled Lower Egypt, while high priests of Amon succeeded the last of the Ramesside kings and held sway over Upper Egypt. The nation now entered upon a chaotic period. Although it would enjoy occasional eras of prosperity and unity, never again would it be a world power.

The bounty of the Nile, which had assured Egypt its wealth, had always aroused the envy of less fortunate neighbors. So long as the nation retained sufficient power to guard its frontiers it had little to fear from these covetous enemies. But in the process of taking these precautions, Egypt laid itself open to internal overthrow. For long years it had assigned much of the task of manning the desert bulwarks to foreign soldiers. Many of these mercenaries were Libyans who were paid in land grants on which they settled with their families. Profiting from a period of divided rule, the Libyans increased their power in Lower Egypt until they rivaled in power the priests in Thebes and the court in Tanis.

Around 950 B.C. one of these Libyans, named Sheshonk, seized control over both Upper and Lower Egypt. The change was made with a minimum of confusion or resistance. Sheshonk could hardly be called a foreigner, for he came of a family of high priests that had lived in Herakleopolis for many generations. At the outset, Sheshonk's regime seemed promising. With considerable energy, the 22nd Dynasty set about restoring Egyptian

A SACRED FALCON *guards a temple at Horus built at Edfu by the Ptolemaic kings. The Ptolemies, last of ancient Egypt's kings, came to rule in the Fourth Century B.C. and reigned until the Roman conquest in 30 B.C.*

prestige. Sheshonk embarked on a foreign policy of conquest. He invaded Palestine, which under King David had become a power to be reckoned with. Taking advantage of the civil war that followed the death of David's son Solomon, Sheshonk raided a number of Palestinian cities and about 930 B.C. plundered the Temple of Solomon in Jerusalem. At home the economy prospered.

But under Sheshonk's son, rivalry between the powerful priests at Thebes and the court began to undermine the Libyan Dynasty. By 730 B.C., civil wars were occurring regularly and local princes were asserting their autonomy. Egypt, splintered and helpless, was an inviting target for invasion.

Once again, when interlopers came they were scarcely strangers to Egypt. Indeed, the Nubians from below the Fourth Cataract who now took over the country were in a sense as Egyptian as the Egyptians themselves.

Upper Nubia had been within the pharaohs' orbit since the time of the New Kingdom, and its culture had become largely Egyptian. Following the last, hapless days of the New Kingdom, Nubia broke away and became independent. A few centuries later it mustered the strength to conquer its former overlord: about 730 B.C., Nubians stormed across the border to dominate most of Egypt. The Nubians, orthodox in their religious observance, brought with them the puritan atmosphere of an older Egypt, the source of their religion, and the strict, theocratic ways of Napata, their small-town capital on the Fourth Cataract. To Nubian eyes, the Egypt they now encountered must have appeared worldly, lax and impious.

Nubian control, concentrated in the area of Thebes, lasted only 70 years. Almost from the time the newcomers took over, they found themselves threatened by bloodthirsty conquerors from the east. Egypt had long been invulnerable to attacks by envious neighbors. For centuries its rich copper mines had guaranteed a supply of the vital war material that gave an era its name: the Bronze Age. When iron weapons came into wide use in the middle of the 12th Century B.C., bronze armaments became obsolete. Lacking iron ore, the Egyptians could now be challenged by other powers which had equal access to this metal, which was unmatched for the fashioning of arms.

Of all Egypt's iron-armed neighbors the Assyrians were perhaps the fiercest warriors. In 663 B.C. they finished off 80 years of intermittent warfare with an overwhelming invasion. There was not much doubt about the issue. As the Assyrians had once warned the Israelites (at a time when the latter were looking to Egypt for military support): "Lo, thou trustest in the staff of this broken reed." The Assyrians, coming down "like the wolf on the fold," stormed all the way to Thebes to end the rule of the Nubians, who withdrew to their own land and in time abandoned Egyptian ways.

The Assyrians enjoyed their triumph only briefly. Within a short time a wily Egyptian prince, brilliant, lucky and shrewd, had tricked the conquerors into departing. His name was Psammetichus, and he managed to convince the Assyrians that they could more profitably rule Egypt through a native nobleman than by instituting military government. The nobleman he had in mind was, of course, himself. Once the Assyrians had withdrawn their troops, they were out of Egypt for good. They became occupied with other matters; meanwhile Psammetichus established a remarkable dynasty, the 26th, with his birthplace as its capital, and Egypt entered a period of relative tranquillity and prosperity.

The secret of Psammetichus' domestic success lay in his talents in the marketplace. In the manner of a modern chamber of commerce, he invited Syrians, Jews, Ionian Greeks and other profit-minded peoples to settle down in Egypt and develop the nation's trade. Egypt became a leading exporter of grain. For centuries thereafter, the crops grown along the Nile were to be a vital element in feeding the Mediterranean area. Political control of this granary became the key to world dominance, and as a consequence a series of powerful nations henceforward would strive to exercise authority over Egypt.

When Psammetichus died after a reign of 54 years, he was succeeded by his son Necho II, who was as shrewd as his father. Hoping to enhance Egypt's role as middleman in the trade between the Mediterranean and the distant east, he began to dig a canal from the Red Sea to the Nile to provide an all-water route for this profitable traffic. Forced to abandon the project because the techniques available to him were not equal to the brilliance of his plan, he cast about for an alternative and conceived the idea of circumnavigating Africa. He equipped an expedition, manned it with Phoenician sailors and sent it off to explore the feasibility of the route. The voyage was successful, but the time it took—three years—could not have been very encouraging; the world had to wait until the 15th Century A.D. for Vasco da Gama to open up an all-sea route to Middle Eastern waters.

The use of Phoenician sailors was typical of the 26th Dynasty's reliance on foreigners for many important jobs: Phoenicians did Egypt's exploring; Greeks and Syrians conducted overseas business; Israelites built a thriving colony at the frontier on the First Cataract; and Greek mercenaries served Egypt in Nubia (among other things, they carved a record of their exploits on one of Ramses' colossal statues, a custom followed by military expeditions since time immemorial).

The 26th Dynasty gave Egypt an Indian summer of independent rule that lasted almost a century and a half. It was brought to an end by a new invasion. In 525 B.C. the Persians overran Egypt and incorporated it into their growing empire. They maintained their dominance (except for brief periods when the Egyptians gained temporary freedom) for two centuries. And then the Persians were themselves humbled by that most spectacular of conquerors, Alexander the Great.

Alexander, who had firmly established Macedonian hegemony over the Greek city-states, entered Egypt in 332 B.C. during the campaign that ended with the destruction of the Persian empire. Following the conciliatory policy he had previously established in Greece, he retained much of the Egyptian administrative system, but he kept ultimate power in his own hands through firm military and financial controls. Though the youthful conqueror stayed only briefly in Egypt, before leaving he decreed the founding of a new city at the westernmost mouth of the Nile. Alexandria was to become a pre-eminent commercial center and the intellectual capital of the eastern Mediterranean. Later, as a meeting ground for early Christian and pagan beliefs, it was to make a profound contribution to the development of Christian theology.

Upon Alexander's death in 323 B.C., his lieutenants parceled out the administration of the empire among themselves. Egypt fell to the lot of Ptolemy, a veteran soldier who had served Alexander as trusted field commander. He established a dynasty that lasted almost 300 years, until the celebrated moment in 30 B.C. when Cleopatra, last of the Ptolemies, pressed an asp to her bosom.

The earlier Ptolemies, hard-headed businessmen, ran Egypt like a corporation, strictly for profit. Greeks themselves, they brought in great numbers of their compatriots to help run the nation. They settled Greek soldiers throughout the country to guarantee stability and to provide an army in time of war. They imported Greek experts to increase agricultural production, and Greek civil servants to staff their administration. By and large, Egyptians

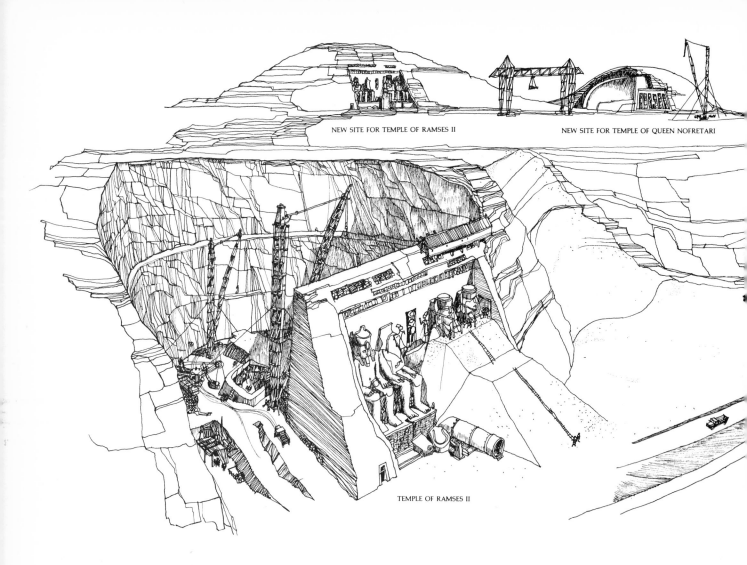

NEW SITE FOR TEMPLE OF RAMSES II   NEW SITE FOR TEMPLE OF QUEEN NOFRETARI

TEMPLE OF RAMSES II

were treated as second-class citizens, although some eventually managed to gain high posts. Under the strict rule of the Ptolemies, the peasants had to work harder than had their forefathers, and they did so sullenly and resentfully. There are records of strikes even in the early years of Ptolemaic rule. After 217 B.C., persistent native revolts finally forced the Ptolemies to make concessions.

Notwithstanding their interest in economics, the Ptolemies, as good Greeks, felt it necessary to sponsor activities of the mind. A Hellenistic culture flourished in Alexandria, a city whose museum and library were famed throughout the ancient world. In Alexandria were gathered the world's leading scientists, poets, artists and scholars—and although their principal purpose was to increase the luster of the royal court, it was through their efforts that scholarship as the West knows it sprang up. It was at Alexandria that Euclid wrote his *Elements*,

that Eratosthenes calculated the circumference of the earth, and that the physician Herophilus pioneered in the study of anatomy.

But the Greek domination of Egypt did not long survive the decline of Greece itself. By 200 B.C. the great new power of the Mediterranean, Rome, began swallowing up the ancient peoples of the East one by one. Inexorably, the influence of the Roman Empire spread to Egypt. The events by which the ancient kingdom actually passed into the hands of Augustus, Rome's mighty leader, form a dramatic chronicle that belongs as much to literature as to history.

Cleopatra, the seventh Ptolemaic Queen to bear that name, was about 18 years old in 51 B.C. when she came to the throne that she shared with her brother, Ptolemy XIII (who, following the royal Egyptian custom, was also her husband). By then, Rome was frequently intervening in the politics of

A DRAMATIC RECONSTRUCTION, *intended to save the vast temple complex at Abu Simbel from inundation, was begun in 1964 as the rising waters of the Nile started to back up behind the Aswan High Dam. In this drawing, which illustrates several stages of the delicate operation, the huge temple of Ramses II is shown being cut away from the cliff, sliced into movable blocks and reassembled on nearby high ground (top of drawing) about 200 feet above the old water level. The small temple of Nofretari is also shown reassembled on top of the hill. At the right of the sketch is the high cofferdam built to hold back the Nile during excavation.*

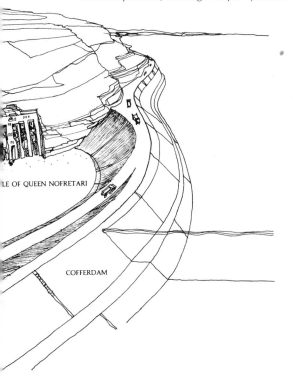

LE OF QUEEN NOFRETARI

COFFERDAM

Ptolemaic Egypt, and contenders for the throne sought Roman approval. The power struggles on the banks of the Tiber became matters of extreme importance on the Delta of the Nile. From their position in the wings, the Ptolemies must have been fascinated by the mortal conflict between Pompey and Julius Caesar for the prize of Roman leadership. Anxious to ally themselves with a winner, the Ptolemies arranged to have Pompey murdered when he turned up in Egypt seeking refuge. Shortly thereafter, the victorious Caesar arrived. Cleopatra very soon became the mistress of Caesar and shared his triumphs until he was assassinated in 44 B.C.

Once again a watcher on the sidelines, Cleopatra waited for the outcome of the resulting fight for power between Caesar's principal heirs, Antony and Augustus. She finally gambled on Antony, the man she thought invincible. But Antony was overcome at Actium by the forces of Augustus, and the defeated Roman fell upon his sword to avoid the humiliation of execution. According to romantic legend he was carried dying to Cleopatra, who thereupon committed suicide by pressing an asp to her breast. That is the legend; all that is known for sure is that she killed herself when faced with the prospect of being taken to Rome as a prisoner by Augustus. Egypt, no longer independent even in name, became a subject province of Rome; Augustus actually treated the conquered land as his private estate, forbidding even senators to visit there without his permission.

Roman organization and efficiency not only restored the businesslike administration of the Ptolemies but added a new dimension of ruthlessness. The Ptolemies had at least lived in Egypt, and the money they exacted had stayed in the country. The Romans, on the other hand, were absentee landlords who milked Egypt mercilessly through agents. The gap between the rulers and the ruled grew wider. Among the Egyptians the sullenness of Ptolemaic days gave way to despair.

Under such unpromising circumstances, Egypt was once again able to leave its mark upon history. The First Century B.C., and the several centuries that followed, was an age in which people throughout the Mediterranean world were in desperate search of a religious experience that could offer them some hope and comfort. The story of the great Egyptian deities—Osiris, the King who had died and been resurrected; Isis, the wife who by her unswerving faith and love had made the resurrection possible; and Horus, the son whose steadfast support had avenged his father's wrongs—proved to possess universal appeal. The emphasis on immortality in the worship of this ideal family trinity gained numerous devotees throughout the length and breadth of the Roman Empire, from the ancient Near East to far-off Britain.

But though this international cult endured for some centuries, it was doomed by the birth of a new religion in neighboring Palestine. By the Fourth Century A.D., Isis and the whole pantheon of Egyptian deities had fallen before a triumphant new rival, Christianity. As the new creed swept around the Mediterranean, one of its first stopping places was Egypt, and the ancient and exhausted land provided the inspiration for several features of incalculable importance to the young and vigorous religion.

Christianity had first trickled into Egypt through that land's Jewish communities around the First Century A.D. In the early days it was addressed primarily to the uneducated masses. But there developed in Alexandria, the nation's intellectual capital, a group of Christian thinkers—including the Greek-born Clement, and the Egyptians Origen and St. Athanasius—who helped provide the young religion with its first systematic theology. These three are considered to be among the most influential of the early Church Fathers.

Alexandrian Christianity was a religion of controversy; the theological disputes that arose around the Fourth and Fifth Centuries resulted in great violence. In one of them, over the question of Christ's divine nature, Egyptian monks, wild-eyed and illiterate for the most part, flocked into the cities from the desert to argue the issue with fists and cudgels. In 415 a mob of Christian fanatics in Alexandria attacked a Neoplatonic philosopher named Hypatia—known for her beauty as well as her learning—and tore her limb from limb.

The monks of Egypt were Christianity's first; later travelers spread the seeds of monasticism throughout Europe—first to Constantinople, then to Rome, and ultimately to the rest of the continent.

Egypt's long and vital connection with Christian thought came to an abrupt halt in 642 A.D., when the governors representing the Eastern Roman Emperor were driven out by Moslem Arabs, then in the full tide of the great conquest that was to make Islam one of the most important of Christianity's rivals. The Nile grain and the Nubian gold that had once gone to Rome and Constantinople now went to Mecca, Damascus and Baghdad. The Arabs ruled Egypt for almost nine centuries, long enough to transform the land completely into an Arab country. They were succeeded by the Turks and finally by the British. Not until the 20th Century did Egypt fully regain its long-lost independence.

When Alexander and Napoleon—both men with a sense of destiny—led their armies into the land of the pharaohs, each was acutely aware that he was stepping upon soil that occupied a very special place in history. It was in the Valley of the Nile that man first created a great state, that he first devised the political institutions to rule a widespread geographical area, first organized the governmental machinery to administer hundreds of miles and thousands of people, first planned and executed large-scale projects. It was in the Valley of the Nile that man achieved a way of life that included not only work and duty but leisure and grace, gaiety and sophistication, magnificent architecture, enduring art. Along with this way of life he created its natural counterpart, a secular literature—essays on how to succeed in life, discussions of the state of the world, short stories of adventure, songs of love.

As Napoleon drew up his soldiers for the Battle of the Pyramids, he addressed to them the celebrated words, "Soldiers, from the summit of yonder pyramids, forty centuries look down upon you." Forty, we know now, was an understatement—and so, for all its grandiloquence, was the rest of the sentence. Those centuries, it is now apparent, do more than merely look down upon us: they are tightly woven into the fabric of Western civilization.

THE FIRST ROOM *of the tomb was reached by clearing a 25-foot corridor, above, of heaped rubble.*

TUTANKHAMEN'S TREASURE

For more than a score of centuries, archeologists, tourists and tomb robbers have searched for the burial places of Egypt's pharaohs. Almost none of these tombs, storehouses of treasure, went undisturbed. Yet, in the Royal Valley, where pharaohs were buried for half a millennium, one tomb was virtually forgotten. This was the now-famous tomb of King Tutankhamen, discovered at last in 1922. The son-in-law of the fabulous Queen Nefertiti, Tutankhamen was a singularly unimportant ruler about whom very little is known. It is estimated that he was only 10 when his reign began about 1361 B.C.; that he married a girl of 12; and that he died at the age of 19. Nonetheless, because Tutankhamen's tomb was found nearly intact, it remains the world's most exciting archeological discovery—and the greatest testament yet found to the quality of ancient Egyptian life.

THE LONG SEARCH FOR A FORGOTTEN TOMB

The British archeologist Howard Carter was nearly alone in his faith that Tutankhamen's tomb could be found. Privately financed and armed with only a few scraps of evidence—among them some seals of the King—Carter dug endless trenches in the Royal Valley, cleared rubble and searched in dumps. It was only after six straight years of digging that he finally unearthed the door of the tomb. "Twice before," he said, "I had come within two yards of that first stone step." He opened the chamber—and beheld in the ancient darkness "strange animals, statues, and gold—everywhere the glint of gold."

THE ANNEX, *containing relics as varied as ivory game boards and boxes of funerary figures, was found in a disordered state, exactly as ancient thieves had left it.*

EXAMINING A COFFIN, *Howard Carter brushes dust off the gilt wood. It took Carter about eight years to remove, catalogue and carefully restore the more than 2,000 objects found in Tutankhamen's tomb. Carter died in 1939.*

THE INNERMOST ROOM *housed an immense gilded wood chest (at far end) containing the dead King's viscera. In front, a jackal-god sits on a gilt chest full of jewels and sacred objects such as scarabs and amulets.*

GLITTERING SPOILS FOR TOMB ROBBERS

About 10 years after Tutankhamen's death, thieves broke into his tomb and ransacked the antechamber shown here. But the tomb, resealed and eventually covered over with rubble, was not touched again until modern times—although by 1000 B.C. every other sepulcher in the Valley had been robbed.

Few sites in the ancient world held as much wealth as the Royal Valley, and nearby villagers made a profession of robbing the tombs almost be-fore the doors were sealed. The laborers who built the tombs—and even high officials—shared in the plunder. In a vain attempt to safeguard the royal burial chambers, architects sank the crypts deep into secret recesses and sealed tomb entrances. But despite armies of guards, and watchmen who made regular checks to see that the crypts were sealed, the tombs were violated. Thieves stole anything they could get—even the statues of gods they worshiped.

THE PLUNDERED ANTECHAMBER *had been despoiled of small, easily carried booty. The vast treasure that remained included chests full of linen, caskets, statues, and two dismantled, gilded chariots.*

A STRIPPED STATUE, *this wooden bust of Tutankhamen was probably dressed with rich necklaces and earrings, and later denuded by tomb robbers. The crown is decorated with a carved royal cobra.*

TUTANKHAMEN'S THRONE, *resting on carved lion's paws, is sheathed with gold and inlaid with colored glass paste and semiprecious stones.*

SYMBOLS OF ROYALTY

A pharaoh who was ready for the afterworld was buried amid symbols of his might. Tutankhamen's tomb was full of such objects—many, such as his throne, simply taken from the palace. Most of the furnishings attest to the Pharaoh's exalted power. Although the young Tutankhamen probably never saw a battlefield, one small medallion honors his official (if not actual) prowess as a soldier. Amid the signs of impersonal pomp there are also occasional domestic touches—for example the picture on his throne *(left)* of young Queen Ankhesnamum making a wifely adjustment of the King's costume.

A CEDARWOOD CHEST *was carved with hieroglyphs of the King's name and titles. Symbols of life and fortune form the openwork.*

A MARTIAL EMBLEM *depicts Tutankhamen as if returning from war, preceded by captives and followed by a serpent goddess.*

OLDEN UNGUENT BOX *shows Tutankhamen twice, seated under sun. Inlaid feathers, framing sun disks, surmount the lid.*

TRAPPINGS OF LIFE
FOR A DEAD KING

When Tutankhamen's mummy was sealed away in its tomb, the priests saw to it that the dead King, reawakened, would find about him all the accustomed comforts and accoutrements of palace life. They supplied the tomb with over 100 baskets of fruit to feed him, feathered fans to cool him, statues of servants to wait on him. There were an exquisite centerpiece; a beautiful vase to hold oils; two finely wrought ceremonial knives, probably intended for a royal military expedition. As added equipment for such an expedition, the priests buried two chariots and even a folding camp bed.

Besides such traditional objects of royal pleasure, Tutankhamen's tomb contained some special mementos of the young King's childhood. Included among these were a toy-box and a painting set.

AN ORNAMENTAL BOAT *served as a centerpiece. In the prow, a young girl clasps a lotus blossom to her breast; in the stern, a dwarf poles the boat.*

ROYAL DAGGERS, *one gold (top), another iron, were among many buried weapons. The shiny iron blade, over 3,000 years old, showed only specks of rust.*

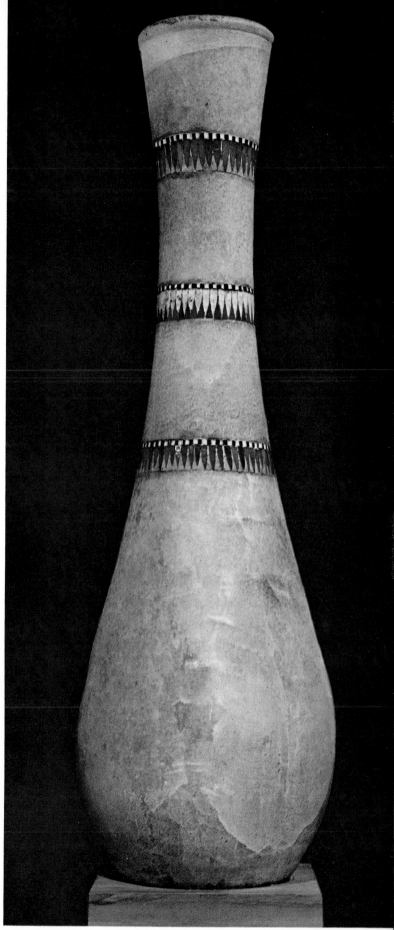

AN ALABASTER VASE *inlaid with floral garlands was once filled with costly oils. Skin oils were provided for the Pharaoh's continued good grooming.*

A WOODEN LIONESS, *this gilded and gessoed beast inhabited the tomb's antechamber. The entire figure, standing six feet long, was designed as a bier.*

BEASTS OF THE TOMB

Many kinds of animals represented gods to the ancient Egyptians and were often kept in temples. They were also favorite subjects for Egyptian artists and craftsmen. Both household and tomb furnishings were decorated with animal figures: a bed or a bier commonly had a lion's head and tail as endpieces, and stood on sculptured paws. The cow Hathor, here forming the endpiece of a couch, had a special place in a pharoah's tomb, for she was sometimes depicted in Egyptian art as suckling a king. Most important was the jackal guarding Tutankhamen's mummy: this creature represented Anubis, god of embalming and protector of the dead.

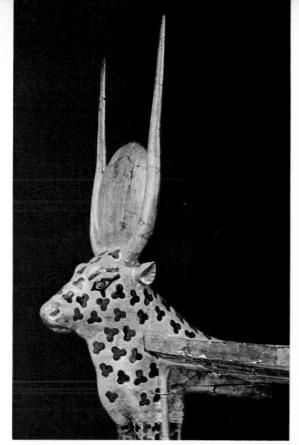

A GILDED COW, *representing the goddess Hathor, has lyre-shaped horns holding a shining sun-disk, a sacred symbol.*

A VARNISHED JACKAL *with silver claws, guardian of the tomb's depths, represented a god known as "He who belongs to the mummy wrappings."*

WITH MACE AND STAFF, *a life-sized statue of King Tutankhamen (about five feet six inches tall) stands beside the door of the burial chamber. The black figure of the Pharaoh is adorned with bright stones and gilt sandals.*

ANCIENT SENTINELS OF THE AFTERLIFE

Not only was Tutankhamen's tomb adorned with gods in the guise of animals, but divinities in human form also stood guard. Two statues of Tutankhamen himself (for pharaohs were considered gods as well as kings) flanked the entrance to the burial chamber. Inscriptions proclaimed that the young Pharaoh was "The Good God of whom one can be proud, the Sovereign of whom one boasts."

In the innermost room, guarding a shrine containing the dead King's vital organs, stood four beautiful goddesses: Isis, protecting the liver; Nephthys, the lungs; Neith, the stomach; and Serket, the intestines. These organs were preserved in separate urns. The heart was left in the mummy.

A DEATHLESS MONARCH LYING IN STATE

Greater than all the treasure in the tomb's outer rooms was the mummy itself, enclosed in its massive interior shrine. Archeologists had never before unearthed a royal mummy still encased in its original state. The mummified King was locked away at the center of a series of cases, each fitting inside another like Chinese boxes—four outer shrines of gilded wood; then a sculptured stone sarcophagus; then three inlaid coffins, the innermost, weighing 242 pounds, of solid gold. Each coffin was shaped in the figure of the King *(right)*. Each depicted him wearing a crown composed of the Vulture and Cobra, the symbols respectively of Upper and Lower Egypt. Even within the final coffin *(below, right)*, the face of the mummy was concealed by a beaten-gold mask *(below, left)*.

"For a moment," reflected the archeologist who unsealed these ancient coffins, "time as a factor in human life has lost its meaning. . . . The very air you breathe, unchanged through the centuries, you share with those who laid the mummy to its rest."

CROSSROAD CIVILIZATIONS BETWEEN EAST AND WEST

The chart at right is designed to show the duration of ancient Egyptian culture, which forms the subject of this volume, and to relate it to the others in the Crossroad group of cultures that are considered in one major group of volumes of this series. This chart is excerpted from a comprehensive world chronology which appears in the introductory booklet to the series. Comparison of the chart seen here with the world chronology will enable the reader to relate the Crossroad civilizations to important cultures in other parts of the world.

On the following two pages is printed a chronological table of the important events that took place within the land of Egypt during the period covered by this book.

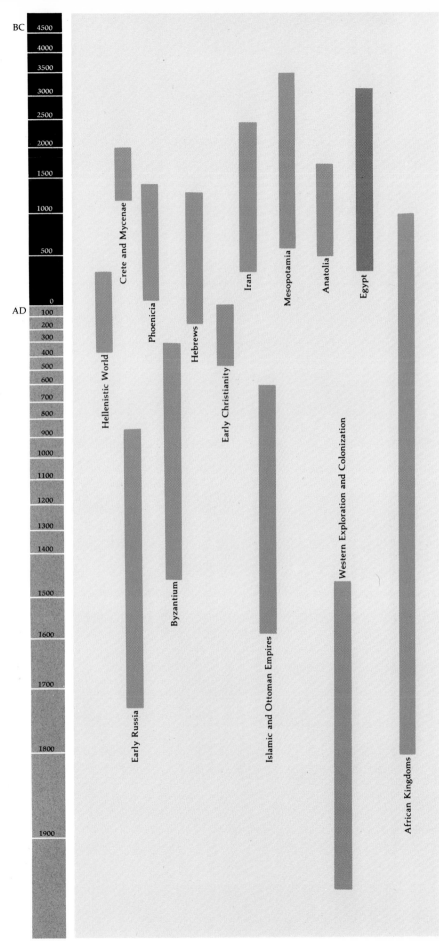

CHRONOLOGY: *A Listing of events significant in the history of ancient Egypt*

EXACT DATING OF EVENTS AT THIS REMOVE IN TIME IS ALMOST IMPOSSIBLE. DATES USED HERE ARE APPROXIMATIONS BASED ON THE MOST RECENT STUDIES.

B.C.	Periods	Dynasties	Politics and Trade	Culture and Society
3200				
3100	EARLY DYNASTIC PERIOD 3100–2686	Dynasty I 3100–2890	Upper and Lower Egypt are united by Menes, the first Pharaoh, who builds his capital at Memphis	Development of calendar and hieroglyphic writing
3000			Trade with Levant	Copper tools and weapons in use
2900			Expeditions to Sudan	Royal tombs built near Abydos and Memphis
2800		Dynasty II 2890–2686	Large irrigation and drainage projects are undertaken	First known treatise on surgery
2700			Religious and political strife between Upper and Lower Egypt	Granite and slate statuary in use
			Reunification under Pharaoh Khasekhemwy	Increased use of stone in building
2700				Skillful metal, ivory, wood and faïence work
2600	OLD KINGDOM 2686–2181	Dynasty III 2686–2613	Djoser is outstanding ruler of this period	Large-scale building and sculpture in stone
			Lower Nubia under Egyptian rule	Step Pyramid built at Sakkarah
2500		Dynasty IV 2613–2494	Outstanding Pharaohs are Khufu, Khafre and Menkaure	Bent Pyramid of King Snefru built at Dahshur
			Wars waged against Nubians and Libyans; timber imported from Lebanon; copper mined in Sinai	The Great Pyramids and the Sphinx built at Gizeh
2400		Dynasty V 2494–2345	Gold and incense imported from Punt	Rise in importance of Heliopolis and its patron, the sun god Re
			Weakening of pharaoh's absolute power	Famed Pyramid Texts, records of funerary customs, inscribed in royal tombs
2300		Dynasty VI 2345–2181	Internal strife grows during Pepi II's long reign	Excellent sculpture in wood and stone for private patrons
			Rise of feudal lords leads to anarchy	
2200				Feudal nobles build sepulchers in their own domains
2100	INTERMEDIATE PERIOD 2181–2040	Dynasty VII 2181–2173	Many kings with short reigns; dissolution of royal power; social and political chaos	Ancient artistic tradition disrupted in wake of political turmoil; pyramids ransacked; tombs and statues destroyed
		Dynasty VIII 2173–2160		
		Dynasty IX 2160–2130	Herakleopolitan rulers of Lower and Middle Egypt battle Theban rulers of Upper Egypt	
		Dynasty X 2130–2040		
2000	MIDDLE KINGDOM	Dynasty XI 2133–1991	Reunification of Egypt under Theban Pharaoh Mentuhotep II, who establishes Thebes as capital	Coffin Texts, later funerary writings, inscribed in tombs of nobles
				Artistic renaissance follows restoration of order
				Mentuhotep's mortuary temple built at Deir el Bahri
1900		Dynasty XII 1991–1786	Powerful pharaohs suppress feudal nobles, undertake large irrigation schemes, vigorously exploit Sinai copper mines,	Period of cultural splendor
				Development of portraiture
				Classical period of literature

Timeline (dates B.C.): 1700 · 1600 · 1500 · 1400 · 1300 · 1200 · 1100 · 1000 · 900 · 800 · 700 · 600 · 500 · 400 · 300 · 200

Period	Dynasty	Dates	Historical events	Cultural developments
INTERMEDIATE PERIOD 1786–1567	Dynasty XIII	1786–1633	Decay of central authority; seizure of power by Hyksos kings, who infiltrate from Asia	*Decline of artistic standards and ideas*
	Dynasty XIV	1786–1603		*Disintegration of traditional culture under impact of Hyksos ideas and techniques*
	Dynasty XV	1674–1567	Under Hyksos rule, Egyptians introduced to powerful Asiatic equipment, including horse-drawn chariots	*Improved spinning and weaving; bronze in general use*
	Dynasty XVI	1684–1567	Nubia and Lower Sudan regain freedom	*New musical instruments—lyre, oboe, tambourine*
	Dynasty XVII	1650–1567		
NEW KINGDOM 1567–1085	Dynasty XVIII	1567–1320	Egyptian Pharaoh Ahmose I ousts Hyksos; Thutmose III expands empire to the Euphrates; Other significant rulers: Hatshepsut, Amenhotep IV (Akhenaton), Tutankhamen and Haremhab	*Opulent craftsmanship, thriving literature; Akhenaton fails to impose monotheism; Elaborate tombs in Valley of Kings; temple of Amenhotep III at Luxor; temple of Hatshepsut at Deir el Bahri*
	Dynasty XIX	1320–1200	Pharaohs Seti I, Ramses II maintain Egyptian power, repel Hittite threat; Under Merneptah, military power declines	*Energetic building activity: temple of Ramses II at Thebes; Hypostyle Hall at Karnak; rock-cut temple at Abu Simbel; "Books of the Dead" written on papyrus rolls*
	Dynasty XX	1200–1085	Rule of Ramesside Pharaohs (Ramses III–XI); invasions of Libyans and Sea Peoples repelled; loss of Asiatic dependencies; increasing poverty and lawlessness	*Mortuary temple of Ramses III at Medinet Habu commemorates victories; Tombs at Thebes looted*
LATE DYNASTIC PERIOD 1085–341	Dynasty XXI	1085–945	Egypt divided; kings dependent on Libyan mercenaries	*Completion of Khons temple at Karnak*
	Dynasty XXII	950–730	Kings of Libyan origin	*Era of thriving craftsmanship; Bronze casting perfected; Skilled metal and faïence work*
	Dynasty XXIII	817–730	Invasion of Palestine; Solomon's temple plundered; Growing dissension encourages invasion by Nubians	
	Dynasty XXIV	730–715	Brief rule by Lower Egyptian king concurrent with Dynasty XXV	*Nubian rulers foster study of the past; Beginnings of a cultural renaissance; New realism in sculpture*
	Dynasty XXV	751–656	Rule by Nubian pharaohs; Thebes sacked during Assyrian invasions	
	Dynasty XXVI	663–525	Independence from Assyrians achieved; Strong fleet; active commerce; trade with Greece	*Arts of past imitated; Faultless incised inscriptions*
	Dynasty XXVII	525–404	Persians conquer and rule Egypt; canal from Nile to Red Sea completed	*Darius I of Persia commands codification of Egyptian law*
	Dynasty XXVIII	404–398	Persians expelled with Greek aid; Egyptian king enthroned	
	Dynasty XXIX	398–378	Pharaohs from Delta rule briefly	*Numerous monuments erected by Pharaoh Achoris*
	Dynasty XXX	378–341	Last native pharaohs; reconquest of Egypt by Persians	*Last flowering of native Egyptian art*
PTOLEMAIC PERIOD 332–30			Alexander the Great conquers Egypt; on death of Alexander, one of his generals founds Ptolemaic Dynasty	*Temple of Isis at Philae; Temple of Horus at Edfu; Temple at Kom Ombo; Temple of Hathor at Dendera*

A GALLERY OF THE GODS OF EGYPT

The ancient Egyptians did not think of their deities as abstract and distant beings, but believed that they had the same desires and physical needs as all living things. Gods were sometimes represented as humans, sometimes as animals, sometimes as a mixture of both. It was easy for Egyptians to bring the deities into every phase of their lives; nothing happened anywhere that was not arranged by one god or another.

ISIS, *wife and sister of Osiris, was gifted with great magical powers. Among other good works, she protected children—which made her most popular of Egyptian goddesses.*

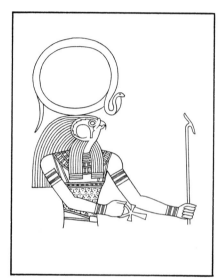

RE, *the sun god of Heliopolis, became a state deity in the Fifth Dynasty. Some traditions made him the creator of men, and the Egyptians called themselves "the cattle of Re."*

ANUBIS, *the jackal-god of mummification, assisted in the rites by which a dead man was admitted to the underworld. He holds the divine sceptre carried by kings and gods.*

NEPHTHYS, *sister of Isis, was a goddess of women. Her name means "Lady of the Castle," and she was associated with the home of Osiris, whom she helped restore to life.*

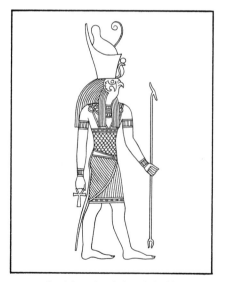

HORUS, *the falcon-headed god, holds in his right hand the ankh, a symbol of life. The kings of Egypt associated themselves with Horus, who was the son of Isis and Osiris.*

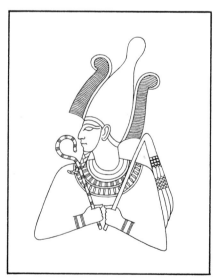

OSIRIS, *a god of the earth and vegetation, symbolized in his death the yearly drought and in his miraculous rebirth the periodic flooding of the Nile and the growth of grain.*

Gods were often merged when political and philosophical fashions changed. For example, during the long period when the cult of Re had official sanction, the compound divinities of Amon Re, Khnum Re and Sobek Re enabled priests to maintain their local cults while paying homage to the state deity. Since there were so many gods, there were bound to be rivalries and contradictions, but the flexible Egyptian religion absorbed them all. Horus, who avenged the murder of his father Osiris, was worshiped but so was Seth, the murderer. This easy tolerance fitted in well with the Egyptians' optimistic belief that "the gods are content and happy of heart, and life is spent in laughter and wonder." Twelve of the most important of the Egyptian deities are pictured below, most of them wearing the distinctive crowns of divinity.

HATHOR, *horned cow-goddess of love, was also deity of happiness, dance and music. When a child was born, seven Hathors came to his bedside to decide his future life.*

SETH *was regarded as the Lord of Upper Egypt and was represented by a big-eared imaginary animal resembling a donkey. He was associated with the desert and storms.*

THOTH, *depicted as an ibis or a baboon, was the god of wisdom and is associated with the moon; as the sun vanished, Thoth tried to dispel the darkness with his light.*

PTAH, *a local god of Memphis, was the patron of craftsmen. Some legends say he spoke the names of all the things in the world and thereby caused them to spring into existence.*

SOBEK, *a crocodile-god, was worshiped in cities that depended on water, such as the oasis city of Crocodilopolis, where the reptiles were kept in pools and adorned with jewels.*

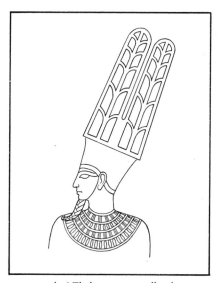

AMON, *god of Thebes, was usually shown as human, but sometimes as a ram or a goose. The Romans later worshiped him as Jupiter Amon and consulted oracles at his temple.*

BIBLIOGRAPHY

These books were selected during the preparation of the volume for their interest and authority, and for their usefulness to readers seeking additional information on specific points.

An asterisk (*) marks works available in both hard-cover and paperback editions; a dagger (†) indicates availability only in paperback.

GENERAL READING

*Aldred, Cyril, *The Egyptians*. Praeger, 1961.
†*The Cambridge Ancient History*, fascicles, Nos. 1-35. Rev. ed., Vols. I and II. Cambridge University Press.
†Childe, V. Gordon, *What Happened in History*. Penguin Books, 1964.
*Desroches-Noblecourt, Christiane, *Tutankhamen*. New York Graphic Society, 1963.
Elgood, P. G., *The Later Dynasties of Egypt*. Oxford, Basil Blackwell, 1951.
†Frankfort, Henri, *Before Philosophy*. Penguin Books, 1959.
*Frankfort, Henri, *The Birth of Civilization in the Near East*. Indiana University Press, 1951.
*Gardiner, Alan H., *Egypt of the Pharaohs*. Oxford University Press, 1961.
Glanville, Stephen R. K., ed., *The Legacy of Egypt*. Oxford University Press, 1942.
†Gurney, O. R., *The Hittites*. Penguin Books, 1961.
*Herodotus, *The Persian Wars*. Transl. by George Rawlinson. Modern Library, 1942.
Kees, Hermann, *Ancient Egypt*. Transl. by Ian F. D. Morrow. University of Chicago Press, 1961.
*Kramer, Samuel N., *Mythologies of the Ancient World*. Doubleday Anchor Books, 1961.
Kramer, Samuel N., *The Sumerians*. University of Chicago Press, 1963.
Lassoe, Jorgen, *People of Ancient Assyria*. Barnes & Noble, 1963.
Posener, Georges, ed., *Dictionary of Egyptian Civilization*. Tudor Publishing Co., 1961.
Smith, William Stevenson, *Ancient Egypt*. Beacon Press, 1961.
*Steindorff, George, and Keith C. Seele, *When Egypt Ruled the East*. University of Chicago Press, 1957.

CULTURE

Breasted, James H., ed. and transl., *Ancient Records of Egypt*. 5 vols. Russell & Russell, 1962.
Davies, Nina M., *Picture Writing in Ancient Egypt*. Oxford University Press, 1958.
Erman, Adolf, *The Literature of the Ancient Egyptians*. Universe Books, 1964.
Gardiner, Alan H., *Egyptian Grammar*. Oxford University Press, 1957.
Hurst, H. E., *The Nile*. London, Constable & Co., 1957.
Riefstahl, Elizabeth, *Thebes in the Time of Amunhotep III*. University of Oklahoma Press, 1964.
*Wilson, John A., *The Burden of Egypt: An Interpretation of Ancient Egyptian Culture*. University of Chicago Press, 1951. (Paperback title: *The Culture of Ancient Egypt*.)

RELIGION

*Breasted, James H., *Development of Religion and Thought in Ancient Egypt*. Peter Smith, 1959.
Cerny, Jaroslav, *Ancient Egyptian Religion*. London, Hutchinson & Co., 1952.
*Frankfort, Henri, *Ancient Egyptian Religion*. Peter Smith, 1961.
Frankfort, Henri, *Kingship and the Gods*. University of Chicago Press, 1948.

Pritchard, James B., *Ancient Near Eastern Texts Relating to the Old Testament*. Princeton University Press, 1955.

ART, ARCHITECTURE AND ARCHEOLOGY

Carter, Howard, and A. C. Mace, *The Tomb of Tut-Ankh-Amen*. 3 vols. Cooper Square Publishers, 1963.
†Edgerton, William F., and John A. Wilson, eds. and transls., *Historical Records of Ramses III*. University of Chicago Press, 1936.
†Edwards, I.E.S., *The Pyramids of Egypt*. Penguin Books, 1961.
Ehrich, Robert W., ed., *Chronologies in Old World Archaeology*. University of Chicago Press, 1965.
*Emery, Walter B., *Archaic Egypt*. Peter Smith, 1963.
Fakhry, Ahmed, *The Pyramids*. University of Chicago Press, 1961.
Hayes, William C., *The Scepter of Egypt*. 2 vols. New York Graphic Society, 1959.
Lange, Kurt, and Max Hirmer, *Egypt: Architecture, Sculpture, Painting in 3,000 Years*. Phaidon Publishers, 1961.
Mekhitarian, Arpag, *Egyptian Painting*. Skira, World Publishing Co., 1954.
†Piankoff, Alexandre, *The Shrines of Tut-Ankh-Amon*. Harper Torchbooks, 1962.
Smith, William Stevenson, *The Art and Architecture of Ancient Egypt* (Rev. ed.). Penguin Books, 1966.
"Victory in Nubia," *The UNESCO Courier* (December, 1964).
Wilson, John A., *Signs and Wonders Upon Pharaoh*. University of Chicago Press, 1964.
Woldering, Irmgard, *Art of Egypt*. Crown Publishers, 1963.

THE SCIENCES

Lucas, Alfred, *Ancient Egyptian Materials and Industries*. 4th ed. rev. by J. H. Harris. St. Martin's Press, 1962.
*Neugebauer, Otto, *The Exact Sciences in Antiquity*. Brown University Press, 1957.
*Sarton, George, *History of Science*, Vol. I. Harvard University Press, 1952.
Sigerist, Henry E., *A History of Medicine*, Vol. I, *Primitive and Archaic Medicine*. Oxford University Press, 1951.
Singer, Charles, E. J. Holmyard and A. R. Hall, eds., *A History of Technology*, Vol. I. Oxford University Press, 1954.
Yadin, Yigael, *The Art of Warfare in Biblical Lands*. 2 vols. Mc-Graw-Hill, 1963.

EGYPT IN PICTURES

Drower, Margaret S., and Roger Wood, *Egypt in Colour*. McGraw-Hill, 1964.
Elisofon, Eliot, *The Nile*. Viking Press, 1964.
Nawrath, Alfred, *Egypt, the Land between Sand and Nile*. Rand McNally, 1963.
*Pritchard, James B., *The Ancient Near East in Pictures*. Princeton University Press, 1955.
Riesterer, Peter P., *Egypt*. Hill & Wang, 1964.

ACKNOWLEDGMENT OF QUOTATIONS

P. 36—Adapted from *Ancient Near Eastern Texts Relating to the Old Testament*, edited by James B. Pritchard, Princeton University Press, 1955. P. 120—Adapted from *Ancient Records of Egypt*, edited and translated by James H. Breasted, Volume II, the 18th Dynasty, The University of Chicago Press, 1906. P. 144-145—Adapted from *Ancient Near Eastern Texts Relating to the Old Testament*, edited by James B. Pritchard, Princeton University Press, 1955.

ACKNOWLEDGMENTS

The editors of this book are particularly indebted to Alan Schulman, Associate Professor of Ancient History, Queens College, New York; Dows Dunham, Curator Emeritus of Egyptian Art, Museum of Fine Arts, Boston; Eric Young, Assistant Curator of Egyptian Art, The Metropolitan Museum of Art, New York; Abdel Moneim El Sawi, Undersecretary of Ministry of Culture, Cairo; Mohamed Mahdi, Director of Department of Antiquities, Cairo; Mohamed Hassan, Director of Egyptian Museum, Cairo; Abdel Kader Selim, First Curator, Egyptian Museum, Cairo; Ramadan Saad, Inspector, Antiquities Department, Luxor; Munir Ismail, Director of Public Relations, Department of Informa-tion, Cairo; Wolfgang Müller, Director, Steffen Wenig, Margarete Wolf and Hannelore Kischkewitz, Egyptian Department, Staatliche Museen, East Berlin; Max Hirmer and H. Müller-Feldmann, Munich; Zentrale Farbbild Agentur, Düsseldorf; Bildarchiv Foto Marburg; Christiane Desroches-Noblecourt, Curator of Egyptology, and the Department of Egyptology, Louvre Museum, Paris; Department of Egyptian Antiquities, The British Museum, London; Ralph Bankes, Esq., London; Silvio Curto, Director, and Maria Rosa Orsini, Museo Egizio, Turin; Ezio Gribaudo, Edizioni d'Arte Fratelli Pozzo, Turin; and Lauro Venturi, Editions d'Art Albert Skira, Geneva.

ART INFORMATION AND PICTURE CREDITS

The sources for the illustrations that appear in the chapters of this book are set forth below. Credits for pictures that are positioned from left to right on a particular page are separated by semicolons; those positioned from top to bottom are separated by dashes. Photographers' names which follow a descriptive note appear in parentheses.

Cover—Statue of Khafre, diorite, Fourth Dynasty, Egyptian Museum, Cairo (Roger Wood, *Egypt in Colour*, published by Thames & Hudson Ltd., London).

CHAPTER 1: 10—Pectoral ornament, gold cloisonné with semiprecious stones and glass paste, from the tomb of Tutankhamen, 18th Dynasty, Egyptian Museum, Cairo (F. L. Kenett, © George Rainbird Ltd.). 13—Lotus and papyrus pillars from temple of Amon at Karnak, granite, 18th Dynasty (Eliot Elisofon). 15—Sketch by Vivant Denon from *Voyage en Egypte*, 1798-1799, New York Public Library. 17—Court of Ramses II at Luxor, 19th Dynasty (Elliott Erwitt from Magnum). 18-19—Sphinx at Gizeh, perhaps representing Khafre, limestone, Fourth Dynasty (Eliot Elisofon). 20-21—Step Pyramid and temple of Djoser at Sakkarah, Third Dynasty (Eliot Elisofon); statue of Djoser, limestone, Third Dynasty (Eliot Elisofon)—pyramids of Khafre (Chephren) and Khufu (Cheops) at Gizeh, Fourth Dynasty (Eliot Elisofon). 22—Statue of Ramses II from his temple at Abu Simbel, sandstone, 19th Dynasty (René Burri from Magnum). 23—Temple of Queen Nofretari with statues of Ramses II and Queen Nofretari at Abu Simbel, sandstone, 19th Dynasty (Ray Garner). 24-25—Temple of Queen Hatshepsut at Deir el Bahri, limestone, 18th Dynasty (Walter Sanders); unfinished head of a woman believed to be Queen Nefertiti, from Tell el Amarna, quartzite, 18th Dynasty, Egyptian Museum, Cairo (Roger Wood, *Egypt in Colour*, published by Thames & Hudson Ltd., London). 26-27—Unfinished statue of Osiris at Aswan, red granite, date unknown (Roger Wood, *Egypt in Colour*, published by Thames & Hudson Ltd., London).

CHAPTER 2: 28—Detail from the Voyage to Punt, painted relief from the temple of Queen Hatshepsut at Deir el Bahri, 18th Dynasty, Staatliche Museen, East Berlin (Erich Lessing from Magnum). 33—Drawings by Otto van Eersel. 34—Diagram by Lowell Hess adapted from *The Nile* by H. E. Hurst, Constable and Company Ltd., London. 37—Tor Eigeland from Black Star. 38-39—Roger Wood Studio. 40 through 49—Tor Eigeland from Black Star, except 44 top—Eliot Elisofon.

CHAPTER 3: 50—Relief detail from Ramses III temple at Medinet Habu, sandstone, 20th Dynasty (Erich Lessing from Magnum). 52—Narmer Palette from Hierakonpolis, schist, First Dynasty, verso, Egyptian Museum, Cairo (Bildarchiv Foto Marburg). 53—Narmer Palette, recto, Egyptian Museum, Cairo (Eliot Elisofon). 55—Head of Queen Nefertiti, painted limestone, 18th Dynasty, Museum Dahlem, West Berlin (Bildarchiv Foto Marburg); head of Queen Hatshepsut, granite, 18th Dynasty, The Metropolitan Museum of Art, New York (Yale Joel)—head of Thutmose III, black granite, 18th Dynasty, Egyptian Museum, Cairo (Eliot Elisofon)—head of Ramses II, black granite, 19th Dynasty, Turin Museum (Bildarchiv Foto Marburg); head of Amenhotep III, basalt, 18th Dynasty, Brooklyn Museum, New York. 58-59—Drawings by Otto van Eersel. 61—Relief detail from Ramses III temple at Medinet Habu, sandstone, 20th Dynasty (Erich Lessing from Magnum). 62-63—Relief details from Ramses III temple at Medinet Habu, sandstone, 20th Dynasty (Erich Lessing from Magnum). 64—Detail from relief on temple of Ramses III at Medinet Habu, sandstone, 20th Dynasty (Erich Lessing from Magnum)—drawing by Otto van Eersel after model of 18th Dynasty chariot, The Metropolitan Museum of Art, New York. 65—Drawings by Otto van Eersel after quiver and bow from wall painting from the tomb of Kenamon at Thebes, 18th Dynasty; sickle sword from the tomb of Tutankhamen, 18th Dynasty, Egyptian Museum, Cairo; ax, 18th Dynasty, British Museum, London; dagger, 20th Dynasty, British Museum, London; detail from relief on temple of Ramses III at Medinet Habu, sandstone, 20th Dynasty (Erich Lessing from Magnum). 66-67—Detail from relief on temple of Ramses III at Medinet Habu, sandstone, 20th Dynasty (Erich Lessing from Magnum)—drawing by Otto van Eersel after relief on temple of Ramses III at Medinet Habu, 20th Dynasty. 68-69—Details from relief on temple of Ramses III at Medinet Habu, sandstone, 20th Dynasty (Erich Lessing from Magnum).

CHAPTER 4: 70—Relief from temple of Ramses II at Abydos, 19th Dynasty (Ray Garner). 73—Cat mummy, Ptolemaic era, The University Museum, University of Pennsylvania, Philadelphia—crocodile mummy mask, Ptolemaic era, The Metropolitan Museum of Art, Rogers Fund, 1912. 75—Statue of goddess Sekhmet, 18th Dynasty, Staatliche Museen, Berlin (Bildarchiv Foto Marburg); statue of god Bes, Ptolemaic era, The University Museum, University of Pennsylvania, Philadelphia; statue of god Thoueris, 26th Dynasty, Egyptian Museum, Cairo (Bildarchiv Foto Marburg). 77—Mummy of Ramses II, 19th Dynasty, Egyptian Museum, Cairo (Elliott Erwitt from Magnum). 78—Wall painting from the tomb of Tutankhamen at Thebes, 18th Dynasty (Eliot Elisofon). 81—Wall painting from the tomb of Ramses VI at Thebes, 20th Dynasty (Eliot Elisofon). 82—Wall painting from the tomb of Nebamun and Ipuki at Thebes, 18th Dynasty (David Lees). 83—Wall painting from the tomb of the vizier Ramose at Thebes, 18th Dynasty (Hassia). 84-85—Painted re-

lief from Thebes, 19th Dynasty, Egyptian Museum, Cairo (Tor Eigeland from Black Star). 86-87—Painted papyrus from a tomb at Deir el Bahri, 21st Dynasty, The Metropolitan Museum of Art (Raymond V. Schoder, S.J.)—painted papyrus from "The Book of the Dead," 18th Dynasty, Turin Museum (from the volume *Museo Egizio*, published by Fratelli Pozzo, Turin). 88-89—Painted papyrus from "The Book of the Dead of Ani," 19th Dynasty, British Museum, London (John Freeman)—Funerary ship, tomb model, painted wood, 12th Dynasty, British Museum, London (Larry Burrows). 90-91—Painting from the ceiling of the tomb of Ramses VI at Thebes, 20th Dynasty (Erich Lessing from Magnum).

CHAPTER 5: 92—Wall painting from the tomb of Nakht at Thebes, 18th Dynasty (Erich Lessing from Magnum). 95—Death mask from Mycenae, gold, c. 1500 B.C., National Museum, Athens. 96—Models of Egyptian soldiers from the tomb of Mesehti at Asyut, painted wood, 11th Dynasty, Egyptian Museum, Cairo (Eliot Elisofon). 98—Objects of various periods, The University Museum, University of Pennsylvania (Henry Groskinsky). 103—Wall painting from tomb of Inherkhau at Deir el Medineh, 20th Dynasty (Erich Lessing from Magnum). 104-105—Drawings by Victor Lazzaro after model of a house at Akhetaton (Tell el Amarna), 18th Dynasty, Oriental Institute, University of Chicago. 106-107—Wall painting from the tomb of Nakht at Thebes, 18th Dynasty (Erich Lessing from Magnum); wall painting from the tomb of Rekhmire at Thebes, 18th Dynasty (Erich Lessing from Magnum). 108-109—Wall painting from the tomb of Menna at Thebes, 18th Dynasty (Erich Lessing from Magnum). 110-111—Wall painting from Tomb of Nebamen and Ipuki at Thebes, 18th Dynasty, British Museum (Derek Bayes)—Wall painting from the tomb of Nakht at Thebes, 18th Dynasty (Erich Lessing from Magnum). 112-113—Painted relief from the tomb of Nenkheftikai at Sakkarah, Fifth Dynasty (Tor Eigeland from Black Star)—Painted relief from the tomb of Mehu at Sakkarah, Sixth Dynasty (Roger Wood, *Egypt in Colour*, published by Thames & Hudson Ltd., London). 114-115—Wall painting from the tomb of Nakht at Thebes, 18th Dynasty (Erich Lessing from Magnum).

CHAPTER 6: 116—Hypostyle Hall from the temple of Amon at Karnak, sandstone, 19th Dynasty (Eliot Elisofon). 118-119—Wall painting from the tomb of Rekhmire at Thebes, 18th Dynasty, copy in tempera by W. de G. Davies, 1926, The Metropolitan Museum of Art, M. M. A. Egyptian Expedition. 121—Drawing by Bob Yasuda of plan of temple of Amon at Karnak, after Baedeker. 123—Block statue of Satepihu, painted limestone, 18th Dynasty, The University Museum, University of Pennsylvania, Philadelphia (David Bridge). 124-125—Draftsman's design, stucco on wood, 18th Dynasty, British Museum, London. 126—Chair, boxwood and acacia, 18th Dynasty, The Metropolitan Museum of Art, Rogers Fund, 1936—Broad collar, gold inlaid with semiprecious stones, Ptolemaic period. The Metropolitan Museum of Art, Dick Fund, 1949. 129-139—Gouache sketches by Nick Solovioff, diagrams by Otto van Eersel.

CHAPTER 7: 140—Detail from the Voyage to Punt, painted relief from the temple of Queen Hatshepsut at Deir el Bahri, 18th Dynasty (Erich Lessing from Magnum). 143—Drawings by Lowell Hess. 144-145—Painted comic papyrus, 20th-21st Dynasties, British Museum, London (R. B. Fleming). 147—Statue of seated scribe, painted limestone, Louvre Museum, Paris (Bulloz). 149—Hieroglyphs from pillar of Sesostris I at Karnak, 12th Dynasty (Hirmer Fotoarchiv, Munich). 150—Rosetta Stone, black basalt, Ptolemaic era with inscription dated 196 B.C., British Museum (Heinz Zinram); Portrait of Jean François Champollion (Culver Pictures, Inc.). 151—Drawings by Lowell Hess adapted from *Cleopatra's Needles and Other Egyptian Obelisks*, by Sir E. A. Wallis Budge, London. 152-153—Drawings by Lowell Hess, except lower right: drawings by Lowell Hess adapted from *Egyptian Grammar*, by Sir Alan Gardiner, London. 154-155—Drawings by Lowell Hess. 156—Hieroglyphs from funerary bed of Queen Hetephras, mother of Khufu (Cheops), gold relief, Fourth Dynasty, Egyptian Museum, Cairo (James Whitmore); Hieroglyphs from the tomb of Queen Nofretari at Thebes, painted polychrome, 19th Dynasty (Raymond V. Schoder, S.J.)—Hieroglyphs from "The Book of the Dead of Ani," Papyrus, 19th Dynasty, British Museum, London (John Freeman). 157—Hieroglyphs from pylon of Thutmose I at Karnak, 18th Dynasty (Eliot Elisofon).

CHAPTER 8: 158—Horus statue at temple of Horus at Edfu, Ptolemaic period (Eliot Elisofon). 162-163—Drawing by Victor Lazzaro after art work by Gunter Radtke, Hochtief, Essen, Germany. 165—Photograph by Griffith Institute, Ashmolean Museum from *Tutankhamen*, by Christiane Desroches-Noblecourt, © George Rainbird Ltd., London, printed by Amilcare Pizzi S.P.A., Milan. 166, 167, 168—Photographs by Harry Burton, The Metropolitan Museum of Art. 169-179—Treasures from the tomb of Tutankhamen, 18th Dynasty, Egyptian Museum, Cairo (photographs by F. L. Kenett, © George Rainbird Ltd.). 184-185—Drawings by Lowell Hess.

INDEX

A

Abu Simbel, *map 9, map 30;* temples of Ramses II and Nofretari, *map 9,* *22-23, 60, 122, *162-163

Abydos, *map 9, map 30,* 79; Osirian pilgrimage to, 79; temple at, 60

Achthoes II, King, 103

Actium, Battle of, 163

Administration, 12, 93-100; civil, 93, 94-96, 99; of conquered lands, 56; Middle Kingdom, 53, 96; military, 93-94, 97-98, 99; New Kingdom, 56, 58, 59, 94; Old Kingdom, 52, 93-94, 95; of provinces, 95-96; of temples, 93, 94, 96-97, 99

Admonitions of Ipuwer, The, 142-143

Adz, *78

Aeschylus, 146

Africa, circumnavigation of, 161

Afterlife, 75-78, 86; concepts and depiction of, 14, 33, 35, 76-77, 81, *88-89, 139; extension to the people, 76, 81, 124; judgment in, 31-32, 81, 86, *87; preparation for, 15, 51, 76, 77, 81, *82, 172. *See also* Immortality

Agriculture, 12, 109, 161; products, *map 30, 32, 102; season, 31; techniques, *40-41, *46-49, *108-109; tools, *40-41; vineyard, *110-111. *See also* Irrigation

Ahmose I, King, 54

Akhenaton (Amenhotep IV), King, 25, 58-59, 60, 101, 127; his "Hymn to the Aton," 145; reform stimulus on arts, 126-127, 142; religious reform attempt, 58-59, 80, 126-127

Akhetaton, capital, *map 8, map 30,* 59, 101

Albert, Lake, *map 30*

Alexander, hieroglyphic name cartouche, *151

Alexander the Great, 53, 161, 164

Alexandria, *map 30,* 146, 161; Christians of, 164; cultural center, 162

Alphabet, 148; Egyptian approach, 141-142, *152-153

Amarna style, 127

Amenemhet III, King, 119

Amenemopet, Instruction of, 144

Amenhotep I, King, 54

Amenhotep III, King, *55, 58, 99, 124, 126; pylon at Karnak, *121; temple at Luxor, *map 9,* 121; temple at Thebes, stele, 120

Amenhotep IV-Akhenaton, King, 58-59. *See also* Akhenaton

Amenhotep-son-of-Hapu, 98-99

Amon, god, 53, 59, 73-74, 80, 90, 99, 120, *185; donation of war spoils to, *68-69, honored at inundation festival, 79; priesthood of, 96, 97, 159; stele inscription to, 120; temples of, 54, 60, 74, *116, 119, 120, *121

Amon Re, god, 74, 144, 185; temple at Karnak, *121

Anatomy, 141, 162

Animal(s): of burden, *37, *47, *109; combined with human forms in religious art, *18-19, *70, 72, 74, *75, *87, *184-185; husbandry, *map 30, 32, *37, *104-105; mummification of, 72, *73; in religion, 43, 71-72, *73, 80, *158, *174-175, 184

Ankhesnamun, Queen, *171

Anthropomorphism, adoption by Egyptians, 72

Antony, Mark, 163

Anubis, god, 71, 72, 77, *87, 175, *184

Apis, sacred bull, 71

Arab rule of Egypt, 164

Arabian Desert, *map 57*

Archeology, 16, 127, 165, 166, 178

Archers, *64-67

Architecture, 13, *20-21, *24-25, *116, 117-122, 128, *158; evolution of pyramid, 118; late period, 122; materials, 13, *20-21, 32, *44, 117-118, *119, 120, 129, *130-131; periods of high activity, 12, 52, 54, 55, 58, 60, 118, 119-122; pylons, 120; temple design, 119-121. *See also* Building; Pyramids; Temples and shrines

Arithmetic, 141, 145-146

Armor, 54, 61, *96

Army, *62, *96; command, 97, 98; foreign mercenaries and conscripts, 60, 63, 68, 102, 159, 161; general conscription for, 61, 97; nonprofessional, 61, 97-98; professional, 58, 59, 61, 93-94, 97, 98, 99; training, 63. *See also* Warfare; Weapons

Art, 13-14, 117-128; Amarna style, 127; basic aims and principles of, 122; combination of human and animal forms, *18-19, *70, 72, 74, *75, *87; comic strip, social satire, *144-145; decline, 127; depiction of daily life in, 35, *103-115, 125; Egyptian influence abroad, 13, 128; foreign influences on, 58, 126; lack of perspective and spatial treatment, 124, 125; reform stimulus of Akhenaton, 126-127, 142; traditionalism *v.* emerging naturalism, 122, 124, 126-127. *See also* Architecture; Crafts; Literature; Painting; Sculpture

Artisans, 93, 100-101, *119, 122; life of, 14, 101; wages of, 101

Asclepius, Greek god, 118

Asia: Egyptian empire in, 12, *map 57;* invasions of Egypt from, 52, 53-54, 160, 161

Assyria, *map 57,* 148; conquest of Egypt by, 160

Astronomy, 141, 145, 146-147

Aswan, 26, 29, *map 30,* 38, 126; lake, 122; stone quarry, *130-131

Aswan High Dam, 23, 60, 163

Atbara River, *map 30*

Aton, god, 59, 80; Akhenaton's hymn to, 145

Atum, god, 74

Augustus, Emperor, 162, 163

Ax, battle, *65

Ay, King, *78

B

Ba, 81, 88, *89

Baboon, in religion, 71, *87, 185

Babylonia, 15, *map 57,* 147; calendar, 146; cuneiform writing, 58, 141

Baghdad, 164

Bahr el Ghazal, *map 30*

Bahr Yusef, *map 8*

Bak, 126

Balcony of Appearances, 15

Banquets, 35, *106-107, *110-113

Bast, 71

Bastet, goddess, 73

Bata, 143

Bent Pyramid, *map 8*

Bes, god, *75, *126

Beverages, 35, 110-111

Bible, 32. *See also* Old Testament

Black land, 31

Blue Nile, 29, *map 30*

Boats. *See* Riverboats; Sailing Vessels; Shipping; Warships

Boats of the dead, 33, *88-89, *138, 139, *172-173

Bookkeeping, 12, 32, 61, 68, 99, *108-109

Bread, *45, 111

Brick. *See* Mud brick

British rule of Egypt, 164

Bronze, 13, 160

Bronze Age, 95, 160

Bronze weapons, *65, 160

Building: labor, 13, 31, 34, 44, 52, 101, 129, 134; materials, 13, 14, *20-21, 32, *44, 117-118, *119, 120, 129, *130-131; season, 31; techniques, 21, 129, *132-137; tools, 118, 129, *130, *132-133

Bull, sacred, 71

Bureaucracy, 12, 58, 59, 99-100, 102

Burial. *See* Funeral

Burial places, 75-76, 117-120. *See also* Pyramids; Temples, mortuary; Tombs

Byblos, *map 57*

C

Caesar, Julius, 146, 163

Cairo, *map 30,* 31

Cairo Museum, 16, 77

Calendar, 31, 34, 146, 148

Camels, *37; caravan, *20-21

Canaan, Hebrew conquest of, 95

Canals, 12, 31, 33, *37, *48-49, 52, 53; Nile-Red Sea, attempt at, 161

Capital cities. *See* Akhetaton; Lisht; Memphis; Tell el Amarna; Thebes

Caravan traffic, *20-21, 34

Carchemish, *map 57*

Carter, Howard, 16, *166-167

Cat mummy, *73

Cataracts, Nile, 29, *map 30,* 34

Catch basins, water, 31, 33, 47, 53

Cattle raising, *map 30, 32, *37; stables, *104-105

Cedarwood chest, from Tutankhamen's tomb, *171

Cedarwood imports, 56

Censuses, 99

Centralization, political, 33-34, 51-52, 53, 54. *See also* Administration

Champollion, Jean François, 16, *150, 151, 156

Chariots, 54, 63, *64, 65, 98; in Tutankhamen's tomb, 168, 172

Cheops. *See* Khufu

Cheops Pyramid. *See* Great Pyramid

Chephren. *See* Khafre

China, Shang Dynasty of, 95

Christianity, rise of, 161, 164

Civil wars, 53, 160

Classes, 12, 93. *See also* Social structure

Clay tablets of Tell el Amarna, 58, 148

Clement, 164

Cleopatra, hieroglyphic name cartouche, *151

Cleopatra, Queen, 151, 161, 162-163

Clergy. *See* Priests

Climate, 15; credited with preservation of treasures, 15, 128, 142; rain and drought cycle, 29, 31

Clothing, 35; foreign influence on styles, 58

Cobra, as symbol of Lower Egypt, *167, *178-179

Coffin of Tutankhamen, *166-167, *178-179

Colonnade of Taharqa, Karnak, *121

Colossi of Memnon, *map 9*

Comic strip art, *144-145

Commissioners, imperial, 56

Communication, 32-33

Conscription: of labor, 13, 34, 44, 51, 129, 134; of troops, 61, 63, 97

Conservatism, 15, 122

Constantinople, 164

Copper: imports, 13, 34; mining, 102

Cordage, of papyrus, 32

Cosmetic jars and tools, *98, 128

Court, Pharaohs', 14-15

Cow, in religion, 71, 72, *174, *185

Crafts, 13, 72, 100-101, *126, 127-128; foreign influences on, 58

Creation: concepts of, 74, 75; gods of, 71, 72, 74; written accounts, 142

Crete, 11, 15, *map 57;* trade with, 53

Crocodile, in religion, 71, *185; mummy, *73

Crocodilopolis, 71, 73, 185

Crowns, Pharaohs', *58-59; in depictions of Osiris, 74; double, 54, *59; Hemhemet, *58; of Lower Egypt, *53, *59; of Tutankhamen, *169, *178-179; of Upper Egypt, *52, *58; War, *59

Cuneiform script, 141

Cuneiform tablets, 58

Cyprus, *map 57*

D

Da Gama, Vasco, 161

Daggers, *65; from Tutankhamen's tomb, *172-173

Dakhla Oasis, *map 57*

Damascus, 164

Dams, 37. *See also* Dikes

Danaoi, 60

Dance, *112-113

Danuna, 60

Dashur, *map 8*

David, King of Israel, 160

Death, emphasis on, 14, 75-76, 80, 125. *See also* Afterlife

Decline, 159-164; of the arts, 127; economic, 97, 101; political, 58-60, 159-160; religious and spiritual, 80, 163

Deir el Bahri, *map 9;* funerary monument of Mentuhotep, 118-119; Hatshepsut's temple at, *24-25, 55, 119-120

Deir el Medineh, artisans' village at, 101

Delta, Nile, 29, *map 30,* 32-33, 39; foreign invasions of, 52, 54; economy of, *map 30, 32; origin of term, 29

Democratic spirit, beginnings of, 75, 76, 101, 142-143

Demotic script, 16, 142, 150, 151, 156

Dendera, *map 9*

Denon, Vivant, 15

Desert, *map 8-9,* 15, 31, 34, *38-39; gold

mining, 31; home of the dead, 39, 84; oases, map 8-9, 34, map 57; its significance for Egypt, 11, 29, 34; trade, 34
Devourer of Souls, 86
Dikes, 12, 31, 33, 52, 53
Djoser, King, *20, 21, 52; pyramid and temple at Sakkarah, *20, 21, 52, 118
Double Crown, 54, *59
Drought, season of, 31
Dynasties, 12, 51. See also First, Second, etc., Dynasty

E

Earth, Egyptian concept of, 76
Eastern Desert, map 8-9, 34, 53, map 57
Ebers Medical Papyrus, 148
Economy: cost of pyramids as drain on, 52; decline, 97, 101; drain of funerary rites on, 78; late period, 160-161; products, 32, 34; prosperity of Middle Kingdom, 12, 53; prosperity of New Kingdom, 54, 58; significance of Nile for, 29, 31-33. See also Agriculture; Shipping; Trade
Edfu, map 9; temple of Horus at, map 9, 122, *158
Edwin Smith Surgical Papyrus, 148
Egyptian character and values, 12, 14, 34-36; conservatism, 15, 122; maat, 74-75; pragmatism, 146, 148
Eighteenth Dynasty, 54-59, 80, 127; architecture, 54, 55, 58, 120-121, 122; priesthood, 58, 59, 96; rise of professional army, 58, 93-94, 98
Elements, Euclid, 162
Elephantine, island of, map 30
Eleventh Dynasty, 53, 118
Embalming, 81, 82. See also Mummification
Emergence, season of, 31
Empire, Egyptian, 12, 56, map 57, 58, 94; decline of, 58-60; dilution of pharaoh's authority, 56, 59, 80, 94, 97; fall of, 60, 159; power of gods and priests, 58, 59, 97
Empires outside Egypt, map 57, 95, 160, 161, 162-163
Engineering, 145, 146; irrigation, 47, *48-49; pyramid building, 21, 129, *132-137; quarrying, *130-131
Entertainment, 35, *106-107, *110-113
Eratosthenes, 162
Ethics, 74-75
Ethiopia, 29
Etruscans, 60
Euclid, 162
Euphrates River, Egyptian expansion to, 54, 56, map 57
Excavations, 16, 127, 165, 166, 178
Expansion, Egyptian, map 57; to Euphrates, 54, 56, map 57; beyond Fourth Cataract, 54; Middle Kingdom, 12, 53; New Kingdom, 12, 54, 56, map 57; into Nubia, 34, 53, 56, map 57, 160; into Palestine, 53, 56, map 57; into Sudan, 56; into Syria, 53, 54, 56, map 57
Exports, 12-13, 32, 34, 161

F

Faïence, *126, 128
Faiyum, map 8, 30
Falcon, in religion, *70, 73, *158, *184
Famines, 31, 52
Fara Fra Oasis, map 8
Farming. See Agriculture; Peasants
Fellahin, 102
Feluccas, *42
Ferrymen, 33
Festivals, 35, 79, 102; religious observances, 77, 79, 102; of inundation, 36, 79
Feudalism, First Intermediate Period, 52, 98
Field of Reeds, 88
Fifth Dynasty, 52, 96, 184
Figurines and models, funerary, 15, 76, *88-89, *96, *167, *172-173

First Dynasty, 33, 51, 118, 125, 128; invention of writing and papyrus paper, 141, *143; King Narmer palette, *52
First Intermediate Period, 52-53, 96, 98, 118; social and religious thinking, 75, 76, 142; writings, 35, 142-143
Fish, sacred, 43
Fishing, 14, map 30, *43, 114
Flood. See Inundation; Nile, flooding of
Flood control, 12, 31, 33, 47, *48-49
Food, 35, 43, *45, *92, 109; left in tombs, 75-76, 77-78, 172
Foreigners, reliance of army on, 60, 63, 68, 102, 159, 161
Fourth Cataract, expansion beyond, 54
Fourth Dynasty, 52, 73, 118, 125
Fowling, 32, *92, *114-115
Frescoes. See Murals
Fuel, lamp and cooking, 32
Funeral, 77, *82-85, *129, *138-139; proper observances important for afterlife, 76
Funerary figurines and models, 15, 76, *88-89, *96, *167, *172-173
Funerary mask, *178
Funerary rites, 77-78
Furniture, 14, *126, 128, 175; in Tut-ankhamen's tomb, *171, 172, 175

G

Galen, 12
Galleys, 67
Gardens, 14, 35, *104-105
Gaza, 56, map 57
Geography, 29, map 30, 31, 33-34
Geometry, 48-49, 146
Gizeh, map 8; Great Sphinx, *15, *18-19; pyramids, map 8, 13, *20-21, 52, 118, 129, 130, *132-139, 146
Gods, 71-75, *90-91, 96, 97, *184-185; abundance of, 72; association with animals, *70, 71-72, *73, *75, 80, *87, *158, *167, *174-175, 184; combining of, 72-74, 90-91, 184; emergence of personal relationship with, 80; folk and local, 72-73, 74, *75; fusion of animal and human forms, *70, 72, 74, *75, *87, *184-185; hymns to, 80; nationwide, 72-74, 80, 185; rise of anthropomorphic, 72; in sculpture and painting, *26-27, *70, *75, *78, *86-91; visible signs given by, 97; worship of, 74, 78-80, *86-87. See also Pharaoh, divinity of
Gold: imports, 13, 56; mining, 31, 102; sources of, 31, 34, 53
Gold dagger, *172-173
Goose, in religion, 73, 185
Government, centralized, 33-34, 51-52, 53, 54. See also Administration
Governors, provincial (district), 52, 53, 95-96, 98, 123, 124
Grain, map 30, 32, 102; exports, 32, 161; harvesting, *41, *108-109
Great Hypostyle Hall, Karnak, 60, *116, *121
Great (Cheops) Pyramid, at Gizeh, map 8, *21, 52, 118, 129, 130, *132-139
Great Sphinx, at Gizeh, map 8, *15, *18-19
Greeks: admiration of, for Egypt, 11; calendar of, 146; conquest of Egypt by, 80, 161; influence of Egypt on sculpture of, 13, 128; Macedonian hegemony of, 161; mercenaries in Egyptian army, 161; Mycenaean civilization, *95; philosophy of, 36, 74; settlement in late Egypt, 160, 161; superseded by Rome, 162; mentioned, 29, 60, 72, 102, 118

H

Haremhab, tomb of, 127
Harmakhis, 18
Hathor, goddess, 72, 175, *185; temple

of, map 9
Hatshepsut, Queen, 24, 54, *55; obelisk at Karnak, *121; her temple at Deir el Bahri, *24-25, 55, 119-120, 121
Hebrews, 11, 36, 80, 160; conquest of Canaan, 95; literary influence on Egypt, 144; settlement in late Egypt, 160, 161
Heliopolis, map 30, 72, 73, 74, 90, 99, 184
Hellenism, 162
Hemhemet Crown, *58
Herakleopolis, map 30, 52-53, 159
Hermopolis, map 30, 71, 74, 90
Herodotus, 32, 51, 52, 77, 82, 112, 134, 148; quoted, 11, 29, 31
Herophilus, 162
Hetephras, Queen, funerary bed of, *156
Hierakonpolis, map 30
Hieratic script, 142, 151, 156
Hieroglyphs, 141-142, 148, *149-157; deciphering of, 16, 149, *150-151, 156; earliest surviving, 152; esthetic effect of, *153, *156-157; latest known, 156; origin of term, 141; reason for loss of meaning, 149
Hippocrates of Cos, 12
History, Egyptian writing of, 12, 15
Hittites, the, 15, 23, 58, 60, 95; empire, map 57
Holidays, 35, 102. See also Festivals
Horus, god, *70, 72, 73, 74, 163, *184, 185; temple of Edfu, map 9, 122, *158
Hostages, foreign royal, 56
Housing, 14, 35, 117; of artisans, 101; middle-class, 14; peasant, 14, *44; upper-class, 14, 35, *104-105
Hunting, 115; fowl, 32, *92, *114-115
Hyksos, the, 53-54, 55, 96, 97, 98, 123
"Hymn to the Aton," 145
"Hymn to the Nile," 36
Hymns, religious, 80
Hypatia, 164
Hypostyle Hall, Karnak, 60, *116, *121

I

Ibis, in religion, 71, 72, *185
Ideograms, 141-142
Iliad, 60
Imhotep, 21, 118
Immortality: general, 76, 81; of pharaoh, 17, 76, 81
Imports, 13, 34, 56, 128
Inscriptions: on block statues, *123; on tomb and temple walls and pillars, 15, *17, 51, 54, 60, *116, 120, 141, 142, *149-151, *156-158
Instruction for King Merikare, 86, 144
Instruction of Amenemopet, 144
Instruction of the Vizier Ptahhotep, The, 36
Intermediate periods, 12. See also First Intermediate Period; Second Intermediate Period
Inundation, season of, 31
Inundation festival, 36, 79
Invasions of Egypt: by Alexander the Great, 161; Assyrian, 160; Hyksos, 53-54; by Moslem Arabs, 164; by Nubians, 160; Persian, 161; Roman, 163; by Sea Peoples, 60, 61, 67
Ionian Greeks, 160
Ipuwer, The Admonitions of, 142-143
Iron Age, coming of, 95, 159, 160
Iron dagger, *172-173
Irrigation, 12, 31, *33, 37, *46-49; labor, 13, 31, 33-34
Isis, goddess, 72, *88-89, 151, 176, *184; internationalization of cult of, 163-164; Temple of, at Philae, map 9, 122, 141
Islam, 164
Israelites. See Hebrews

J

Jackal, in religion, 71, 72, *87, *167, *175, *184
Jerusalem, plundering of Temple of Solomon, 160

Jewelry, *10, 34, *98, *106, *126, 128
Joseph, 31
Julian calendar, 146, 148
Jupiter Amon, 185
Justice, 93, 94-95, 97; punishment, *108-109; social, beginnings of, 75, 142

K

Ka, *81
Kagera River, map 30
Karnak, map 9, 119; Great Hypostyle Hall at, 60, *116, *121; hieroglyphic inscriptions at, *149, *157; inundation festival at, 79; pillars of, *13; temple complex at, 74, 99, *116, 120, *121
Khafre (Chephren), King, 18, 52; pyramid of, map 8, *20-21, 52, 118
Kharga Oasis, map 9, map 57
Khartoum, 29, map 30
Khnum, god, 71, 72
Khnum Re, god, 185
Khufu (Cheops), King, 52, 129, 136, 138; pyramid of, map 8, *21, 52, 118, 129, 130, *132-139
Knives, ceremonial, *172-173
Knossos, 11
Kom Ombo, map 9
Kyoga, Lake, map 30

L

Labor, 31; conscription, 13, 34, 44, 51, 129, 134; construction, 13, 31, 34, 44, 52, 101, 129, 134; farm, 41, 44, 102; misconception about slave, 134; seasonal division of, 31
Landowners, 102; priests as, 97
Law and courts of law, 93, 94-95, 97
Lebanon, trade with, 34, 128
Lesseps, Ferdinand de, 16
Libyan Dynasty, 159-160
Libyans, war with, *61, *68-69
Life after death. See Afterlife
Limestone, uses of, 118, 128, 130
Linen, 34, 143
Lion, in religion, 71, 73, *75, *174
Lisht, map 30; capital, 53
Literature, 12, 15, 142-145, 164; poetry, 36, 144-145; prose, 142-144; wisdom, 36, 86, 144
Livy, 51
Lotus plant, as symbol of Upper Egypt, *13
Lower classes, 35-36, 100-102; chances of advancement, 95, 98-100, 102, 103. See also Peasants; Workers
Lower Egypt, map 8, 29, 32, 47; cobra as symbol of, *178-179; crown of, *53, *59; first unification with Upper Egypt, 12, 51; papyrus as symbol of, *13; Tanis rulers of, 159
Luxor, map 9, 15, map 30; inundation festival at, 79; statues of Ramses II, *17; temple of Amenhotep III, map 9, 121

M

Maat, ethical concept, 74-75
Magistrates, 97
Mariette, Auguste, 16
Marriage, brother-sister, of pharaohs, 54, 162
Mask, funerary, *178
Maspero, Gaston, 16
Mastabas, 117-118
Mecca, 164
Medical papryi, 148
Medical science, 12, 141, 147-148, 162
Medinet Habu, temple of Ramses III, 122; relief carvings, *50, *68-69
Medinet Madi, chapel of Amenemhet, 119
Mediterranean Sea, map 8, 34; Egyptian spheres of influence, map 57; invasions from, 60, 67; trade, 13, 34, 53, 161

Sekhmet, goddess, 73, *75
Senmut, 55, 119-120
Serket, goddess, 176, *177
Serpent, in religion, 74
Servants, 35, 104, *106-107
Sesostris I, King, 149
Seth, god, 72, *185
Seti I, King, 121
Seti II, King, temple at Karnak, *121
Seven fat years and seven lean years, Joseph's prediction, 31
Shādūf, *33, 46
Shang Dynasty, China, 95
Shekresh (Shekelesh; Sikeloi), 60
Shelley, Percy Bysshe, 27
Sherden, 60, 63
Sheshonk, King, 159-160
Shipping, Nile River, *28, 32-33, *42, 43; during inundation, 29. See also Warships
Sicilians, 60
Sikeloi. See Shekresh
Silt, 31
Silver, 13
Sinai, map 8; Egyptian expansion to, map 57; mining, 102
Sinuhe, The Story of, 143
Sirius, 146
Siwa Oasis, map 57
Sixth Dynasty, 52, 118
Slaves, *92, 102, 107, *110; not employed in pyramid building, 134; war, *68, 102
Smith, Edwin, 148
Sobat River, map 30
Sobek, god, 73, *185
Sobek Re, god, 185
Social justice, emergence of concept, 75, 142
Social reform: attempt of Amenhotep IV-Akhenaton, 58-59, 80; unlikeliness of success, 75
Social satire, comic strip, *144-145
Social structure, 12, 31, 35-36, 56, 75, 93-102; and afterlife, 76, 124; chances of advancement, 95, 98-100, 102, 103; and living standards, 14, 35-36, 101-102, *103-115; standing of priests, 79, 96-97. See also Lower classes; Nobles; Officials; Peasants; Upper classes; Workers
Soil, 31
Solar calendar, 146
Solomon, King of Israel, 160
Sophocles, 146
Soul, in afterlife, 76-77. See also Ka
Spears, *63
Sphinx, at Gizeh, map 8, *15, *18-19
Stele inscriptions, 120
Step Pyramid, at Sakkarah, map 8, *20, 21, 52, 118
Stone, kinds used in sculpture and crafts, 120, 128
Stone construction, 13, 21, 118, 119, 129, 130, *132-139; transportation of stones, 118, *130-131, *134-135; weight of blocks, 21, 129
Stone quarry, *130-131
Stones, semiprecious, 34, 128
Story of Sinuhe, The, 143
Strikes, 101, 162

Sudan: Egyptian expansion into, 56; mining, 74, 102
Suez, Gulf of, map 8
Sun gods and worship, 72; Harmakhis, 18; Re, 52, 72, 73, 74, *184, 185
Sun myths, 88, 91
Surveying, 49, *108-109, *132-133
Syria, 14, 60, 148; Egyptian expansion into, 53, 54, 56, map 57; taken by Hittites, 58; trade with, 34, 128; worship of Amon in, 74
Syrians, settlement in late Egypt, 160, 161

T

Taharqa, King, pylon and colonnade at Karnak, *121
Tale of the Two Brothers, The, 143
Tana, Lake, map 30
Tanis rulers of Lower Egypt, 159
Taxation, 12, 31, 94, 99, 109; exemption of priests from, 96-97
Tell el Amarna, map 8, map 30, 104; capital, 35, 59; cuneiform tablets, 58, 148
Temples and shrines, map 9, 17, 74, 84, 119-122; at Abydos, 60; administration of, 93, 94, 96-97, 99; of Amenhotep III, at Luxor, map 9, 121; of Amenhotep III, at Thebes, stele, 120; of Amon and Amon Re, 54, 60, 74, *116, 119, 120, *121; daily ritual in, 78-79; design, 119-122; Djoser's, at Sakkarah, *20, 21; estates of, 58, 97, 99; of gods, 119, 120-122; of Hatshepsut, at Deir el Bahri, *24-25, 55, 119-120, 121; of Hathor, map 9; of Horus, at Edfu, map 9, 122, *158; income of, 78; of Isis, at Philae, map 9, 122, 141; of Karnak, 60, 74, 99, *116, 119, 120, *121; kinds of, 119; of Kom Ombo, map 9; at Medinet Habu, *68-69, 122; of Mentuhotep, at Deir el Bahri, 118-119; mortuary, 119-120, 122; murals, 14, 122, 125 (see also Murals); of Ramses II and Nofretari, at Abu Simbel, map 9, *22-23, 60, 122, *162-163; of Ramses II, at Sebua, map 9; of Ramses II, at Thebes (Ramesseum), map 9, 60, 101, 122; relief carvings, 119-120, 122, 124, 125 (see also Sculpture, relief); sacred animals at, 71-72; at Thebes, map 9, 54, 60, 120
Tenth Dynasty, 52
Thebes, map 9, map 30, 36, 53, 54, map 57, 119, 159, 160; capital, 34, 52-53, 54, 59, 73, 126; god and religious concepts of, 53, 73, 74, 90, 96, 185; necropolis of, 99, 101; temple of Amenhotep III, stele, 120; temple of Ramses II (Ramesseum), map 9, 60, 101, 122; workers' strike at, 101
Third Dynasty, 51-52, 118, 125
Thirteenth Dynasty, 53
Thoth, god, 71, 72, 90, *185
Thoueris, god, *75
Throne, of Tutankhamen, *171
Thucydides, 51
Thutmose I, King, 54, 157; pylons at Karnak, *121

Thutmose II, King, 54
Thutmose III, King, 24, 54, *55, 56-58, 59, 94, 126; pylon and festival hall at Karnak, *121
Thutmose IV, King, 18
Timber, lack of, 32, 128; imports, 34, 128
Timekeeping, 147
Tomb inscriptions. See Inscriptions
Tombs: food left in, 75-76, 77-78, 172; funerary figurines and models in, 15, 76, *88-89, *96, *167, *172-173; furnishings in, 15-16, 128, *167-168, *170-171, 175; location of, 35, 84-85; looting of, 16, 78, 101, 137, *167, 168; murals, 14, 122, 125 (see also Murals); neglect of, 78; of Neolithic Age, 75-76; of nobles, 54, 76; of pharaohs, 17, 51, 52, 54, 76, 79, 117-119, *136-137, *165-179; preparation of, before death, 76; relief carvings, 119-120, 122, 124, 125 (see also Sculpture, relief); tools left in, 16, 75-76, 77; papermaking, *143; water-raising, *33, *46-47; writing, 100, 142. See also Pyramids; Temples, mortuary
Tools and utensils, 37; artistry in, 13; building, 118, 129, *130, *132-133; cosmetic, *98; farming, *40-41; left in tombs, 16, 75-76, 77
Trade, 12-13, 34, 53, 55, 58, 160-161. See also Exports; Imports; Shipping
Transportation: caravan, 34; water, 32-33, *42, 43
Treasurer, 94
Tribes, prehistoric, 11-12, 29, 31, 51
Turkish rule of Egypt, 164
Tursha (Tyrshenoi), 60
Tutankhamen, King, 78, 165, *169-171, *176, *178-179; tomb of, and treasures found, *10, 16, *78, *165-179
Twelfth Dynasty, 53, 120, 128, 143
Twentieth Dynasty, 59-60, 159
Twenty-second Dynasty, 159-160
Twenty-sixth Dynasty, 160-161
Tyrshenoi. See Tursha

U

Uganda, 29
Underworld: gods of, 71, 72, 76, 81; judgment in, 31-32, 81, 86, *87. See also Afterlife
Unguent box, from Tutankhamen's tomb, *170
Uni, vizier, 95
Unification of Upper and Lower Egypt, 12, 51; symbols of, *13, *59
Upper classes, 35, 36, 93, 124; army service, 61, 63; housing, 14, 35, *104-105; life of, 35, 103, *106-107, *110-115. See also Nobles; Priests
Upper Egypt, map 9, 29, 32; crown of, *52, *58; famines, 52; first unification with Lower Egypt, 12, 51; lotus as symbol of, *13; rule of high priests of Amon over, 159; vulture as symbol of, *178-179

Ushebtis, 76. See also Figurines

V

Valley of the Kings, 54, 101, 165, 166, 168
Vases, 128; alabaster, *173
Victoria, Lake, map 30
Villages, 12, *39, *44
Vineyard, *110-111
Vizier, office of, 93, 94-95, 97
Voyage of Wenamon, The, 143-144
Vulture, as symbol of Upper Egypt, *178-179

W

Wadi Halfa, map 30; flooding, graph 34
Wages, 101, 102
War crown, *59
Warfare, 54, *61-67; naval, *66-67; prisoners, 63, *68. See also Army; Weapons
Warships, *66-67
Water clock, 147
Water-raising devices, *33, *46-47
Water supply, 31, *44, 47. See also Irrigation
Weapons, 54, 61, *62-63, *65; bronze v. iron, 160; hunting, *114-115; left in tombs, 16, *172-173
Wells, 31
Wenamon, The Voyage of, 143-144
Western Desert, map 8-9, 34, map 57; burial places, 84
Wheat, 102; harvesting, *108-109
White miter, of Upper Egypt, *52, *58
White Nile, 29, map 30
Wine, map 30, 110-111
Wisdom literature, 36, 86, 144
Women: beauty aids, *98; hairstyles, *110-111; peasant, 40, *44-45; as priestesses, 79-80; property and other rights, 99; as rulers, 24, 54-55; upper classes, 35, 99, 104, *106-107, *110-111
Woodworking, *126, 128, *167, *171
Workers, 12, 14, 93; skilled (see Artisans); strikes of, 101; unskilled, 101
World, Egyptian concept of, 76
Writing, invention of, 12, 141-142, 152
Writing materials and utensils, 100, 142, *143

Y

Young, Thomas, 150

Z

Zoomorphism, 71-72; return to, 80
Zoser. See Djoser

PRINTED IN U.S.A.